CONTEXTUALISATION AND MISSION TRAINING
ENGAGING ASIA'S RELIGIOUS WORLDS

Series Preface

Regnum Resources for Mission provides helpful material to mission practitioners, in both foundational and practical topics.

Regnum Resources
for Mission

CONTEXTUALISATION AND MISSION TRAINING
ENGAGING ASIA'S RELIGIOUS WORLDS

Edited by
**Jonathan Ingleby,
Tan Kang San and Tan Loun Ling**

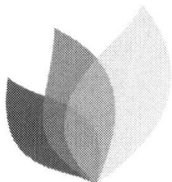

*Regnum Resources
for Mission*

Typeset in Palatino by WORDS BY DESIGN
Photos and cover design by Chara Tan
Printed and bound in Great Britain
for Regnum Books International by 4Edge

The paper used for the text of this book Forest Stewardship Council (FSC) Certified

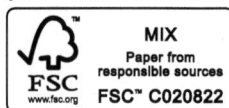

MIX
Paper from
responsible sources
FSC
www.fsc.org   FSC™ C020822

Published by Regnum Books International

regnum

Asia CMS

in partnership with Asia CMS, 10, Jalan 11/9, 46200 Petaling Jaya
Selangor, Malaysia | www.asiacms.net

DEDICATION

To former Redcliffe colleagues and students.

CONTENTS

INTRODUCTION AND ACKNOWLEDGEMENTS

TAN KAN SANG

If the axe is dull
and its edge unsharpened,
more strength is needed,
but skill will bring success (Ecclesiastes 10:10).

Christian missions from the West have had very little success in impacting the religious worlds of Asia. Part of the problem is the lack of serious study of the diversities within Asia's world religions and a general lack of the sort of missiological training which allows students to explore the complex worlds of Islam, Buddhism and Hinduism. Leaders and pastors in many seminaries and churches in Asia stress the need to better equip new workers and mission practitioners so that they are able to appreciate the deep faiths of different religions, and to engage meaningfully with the underlying values and structures of these religions. This will lead to truly authentic disciples of Christ being formed within the heartlands of these communities.

Between 2008 and 2012, CMS, Faith2Share, Global Connections, Redcliffe College, OMF and Wycliffe jointly organised a series of consultations to stimulate the thinking of mission leaders and churches in Britain with the aim to further partnership with the growing Asian mission movements. Selected papers from the first three consultations were published in the book, *Understanding Asian Mission Movements,* (Gloucester: Wide Margin, 2011). These consultations brought together a network of over 120 mission leaders from over 20 agencies and churches in Britain to deliberate on the rise of Asian mission movements and the challenges for partnership in training between mission bodies and churches from Britain and those in Asia.

With the publication of this book on *Contextualisation and Mission Training: Engaging Asia's Religious Worlds*, we offer papers presented at the Fourth Asian Mission Consultation on the theme of Mission Training in Asian Contexts to a wider readership. It is our prayer that this book will partly fill the gap for good mission resources on the theory and practice of contextualisation and how contextual training of mission candidates could prepare a new generation of 'missiologists within Asian religious traditions' who are able to reflect critically on, and engage skillfully with, the multiple religious contexts of Asia.

Although the primary audience of the book is likely to be mission leaders and cross cultural mission workers, we hope that the issues addressed in this book (leadership training, contextualised discipleship, preparation of new workers, the deeper study of Asian religions, interfaith witness) will stimulate local church leaders who are discipling Christian minorities with Asian religious or traditional backgrounds. With the spread of Asian religions to the West, we believe that some of the insights and issues discussed in this book will also be useful for churches in the West in welcoming and reaching out to growing migrant communities.

The first section of the book consists of four different broad 'Frameworks' which could shape and guide Christian approaches toward theological education and mission training. In the second section, 'Engaging the Multiple Religious Contexts of Asia', experienced mission educators present specific explorations (Reviewing Assumptions on Training; The Contextual Approach of Karl Reichelt; The Middle Way Model of Training; and Being Mission in the Indian Context) with regard to the worlds of Islam, Buddhism, Chinese religious traditions and Hinduism. As intended, the papers, when delivered at the Consultation, stimulated controversial responses among participants on how the training of mission workers could enhance deeper and longer term engagements within the complexity of Asian social, cultural and religious systems. It is our prayers that the reading of this book will stimulate further discussion among mission practitioners, students and leaders, those in different contexts of inter-religious engagement around the world.

Together with my co-editors, Jonathan Ingleby and Tan Loun Ling, I would like to acknowledge the organising team for the Consultation: Anton Ponovarev of Faith2Share, Martin Lee and Ann Bower of Global Connections, Peter Rowan from OMF UK, and Hun Kim of Wycliffe International. It was a great joy to serve with a like-minded and energetic team! We also would like to thank each of the authors for their thoughtful contributions. Our sincere thanks go to the leadership at Redcliffe College for hosting the consultations in 2008-2010 as well as to Wycliffe UK for hosting the Fourth Mission Consultation in 2012.

Last but not least, we the editors would like to thank Regnum publication team and especially Dr Wonsuk Ma, Executive Director of OCMS, for their support in publishing these papers for the benefit of a wider readership.

28th June, 2013

WHAT IS SO THEOLOGICAL ABOUT CONTEXTUAL MISSION TRAINING?

TAN KANG SAN[1]

Tan Kang San is Executive Director of Asia CMS. Formerly he was Head of Mission Studies at Redcliffe College, with doctoral work in Islam and Buddhism, and is international consultant on Interfaith issues for the World Evangelical Alliance and the Lausanne Movement.

It helps, now and then, to step back and take the long view.
The kingdom is not beyond our efforts, it is beyond our vision.[2]
(Archbishop Oscar Romero)

Given the rapid growth of Asian missions, what kind of training approaches and models could best prepare Asian workers, especially those crossing traditional, cultural, economic and political boundaries, and how can concerned Christians globally contribute toward the goals and tasks of mission training in Asia?[3] The background for this chapter is my interests and study relating to challenges facing indigenous Christian communities in Asia and the role theological institutions play toward developing contextualised theologies. Asia is incredibly varied and complex. With regard to broad missiological agendas, the Asian church needs to engage in a fourfold dialogue with: Asia's poor, Asia's cultures, Asia's religions, and Asia's cities. None of these complex frontiers could be understood and engaged properly without sustained and substantive theological resources, especially by representative theological communities in each country. Over the last thirty years, there has been a growth of theological discourses with regard to the aims, nature and purpose of theological education in the contexts of intellectual, social, and historical changes, particularly in relation to the crisis of theological education in the West. Firstly, the paper will survey debates on the aims and nature of theological education in the West and highlight key ideas for mission integration. Secondly, we will consider implications for mission training among formal and non formal models of mission training in Asia. Finally, the chapter will explore some programmatic proposals toward a contextual mission training which seeks to grow movements of 'missiologists-in-residence' skilful in reflecting theologically, and critically engaging with Asian mission contexts for the purpose of serving the whole church in their role of prophetic dialogue partners with Asian societies.

The term 'seminary' comes from the old Latin word meaning 'a protected plot of ground for the growth of seedlings' (Stackhouse 1998, 68). For me, the ancient Chinese proverb adds further insight, 'If you are planting for a year, plant grain. If you are planting for a decade, plant trees. If you are planting for a century, plant people.' Mission is about people, and theological training is essentially about helping God's people think clearly about God in order to follow Him in His love for the world. Specifically, good contextual and missional theologies by Asian representative theologians would help the church to think clearly about God's intention for the world, in order to serve alongside God's people and to follow Jesus in his mission in the world. For purposes of this chapter, 'contextual mission' is best expressed through the 'five marks of mission': proclaim the good news of Jesus Christ, disciple new believers, respond to human needs by loving service, transform unjust structures of society, and care for the renewal of creation (Bosch 1991, 519). Missiology is the interdisciplinary study of the salvation activities of the Father, Son and Holy Spirit throughout the world geared toward bringing the kingdom of God into existence; its task is to investigate biblically and critically the motives and methods of mission to see if it fits the criteria of God's kingdom.[4]

FRAGMENTATION OF THEOLOGICAL EDUCATION

This section frames our discussion on appropriate training models within the broader debates on the aims of theological schools by scholars such as Edward Farley, Max Stackhouse and Robert Banks.[5] The future of formal theological education in the West is under threat, as reflected in various literature critiques highlighted in this chapter, the decline of student numbers and the lack of financial support from local churches. The reasons for this decline are complex and are related to the general changes in the intellectual, social and religious developments of theological education. Within Protestant communities, a number of studies on problems associated with theological education in the West have been undertaken. Among others, the following are key factors said to have contributed toward the decline of formal theological training in the West: 1) a lack of value for theological education in the postmodern church (McGrath 1993); 2) professionalisation of theological schools, resulting in a growing gap from the church (Cheesman 2009); 3) fragmentation and loss of integrated purpose in theological education (Farley 1994; Ott 2001); and 4) a lack of missional engagement with society (Stackhouse 1998). 'A missionless church saw no necessity for the inclusion of missiology in the theological curriculum' (Laing 2009, 41-42).

Since the middle of the 1980s, discussions on theological education have moved to a new level, from operational and strategic concerns (how to be more effective) to theological enquiries (why do we do theological education, what are the *telos* and integrative end goals for theological education). Although these studies relate to the situation in the West, some of the findings and conclusions could be of relevance to Asian contexts.

Farley's critiques could be summarised as follow: there has been a shift of understanding theology as habitus, practical wisdom directed to God, to theology as a cluster of disciplines of study (Farley 1994, 80-81; 99-117). By the twentieth century, each field had developed its own specialism and whatever unity between disciplines existed, happened by accident. Subsequently, the emphasis of theological education shifted to a teaching of skills for the professional ministry of clergy (preaching, counselling, pastoral leadership). What is the *telos*, or end of theological education, and what is so theological about theological education or mission training are hardly addressed. Farley criticises this fragmented model by questioning its lack of theological unity, and questions its effectiveness in preparing students for ministry. Farley argues that the aim of all theological education should be *theologia*, or theological understanding (wisdom).[6] According to Farley, integration in theological education can only be achieved through a renewed understanding of theological enquiry as a practical wisdom directed toward God (Farley 1994, 151-171).

It is generally claimed that theological education in Asia inherited the ethos and approach of theological study based on the University model from the West, defined in the fourfold model of theological disciplines: biblical, historical, theological and practical theology as basic disciplines for all theological enquiries (Farley 1994, 110-116; Kelsey 1992, 86-92). In addition to the loss of the internal unity of theological education, and the lack of curriculum coherence, some Asian theologians who received their training in Western schools are influenced by enlightenment thinking: dualism, rationalism, secularism and pluralism (Hwa 2008, 68-70). Bernhard Ott identified the Enlightenment university model of theological education in terms of the following features: 'lack of missionary orientation, academic work in an ivory tower, detachment from the reality of the church in mission, separation of theory and practice, and fragmentation of the curriculum' (Ott 2001, 290). David Bosch found efforts to incorporate missiology as part of theological training unsatisfactory:

> *If mission was studied at all, it was usually as part of practical theology, as if it were largely a matter of technique or practical application; or it was offered as a totally separate subject, as if it had little to do with the other streams, or it is an optional subject, competing with preaching, pastoral counselling, or liturgics for the learners attention (Bosch 1982, 17-19).*

MISSION INTEGRATION IN THEOLOGICAL EDUCATION

Responding to Farley's seminal work, subsequent debates have both challenged and further developed his devastating critique regarding the *telos* of theological education. Bold proposals from Max Stackhouse, Robert Banks, and Bernhard Ott potentially provided theological clarity and impetus for charting new vision and models for contextual mission training in Asia. Due to space limitation, I will highlight their key proposals, those useful for our discussion on developing contextual mission training. Contending with North America's scepticism and pluralism, Stackhouse and his conversation partners were concerned to see theological education as preparing leaders for *apologia* (new cosmopolitan apologetics).

> *(This) can be understood to entail several things: (1) a willingness to enter into the thought forms of those who do not always share the faith assumptions or worldviews that we hold when we enter into dialogue, (2) a willingness to attempt an account of that which we hold most dear in the face of scepticism, doubt and suspicion, (3) a willingness to hear and evaluate on their merits any alternative perspectives that are opposed to our own, and (4) a willingness to*

refute unsound objections to a defensible theological perspective (Stackhouse 1988, 9).

In Asia, the challenge of witnessing and encountering people of other faiths (as a minority community rather than from a position of power) requires a different theological posture and orientation, including acquiring a certain depth of understanding of other religions in order to dialogue with people of other faiths. Unfortunately, at times, our attitudes and evangelistic approaches have been deeply influenced more by Western triumphalistic perspectives than shaped by biblical thinking and accurate understanding of other religions.[7] Stackhouse proposes a bold vision of theological education that advances Christian mission in the context of pluralism and globalisation:

> *Theological education must also claim that the specifically Christian vision of metaphysical-moral reality is normative, can be learned and taught in a disciplined fashion, and is decisive for how other fields of knowledge may be organised, for how every sector of life must be best lived, and for dialogue with other philosophies and religions of the world (Stackhouse 1988, 167).*

For Banks, theological education is a dimension of the mission of the church, supported by Martin Kahler's dictum, that 'missiology is the mother of theology'. It is mission that has the church, not the church that has mission. If it is mission first, then all expressions of specialised ministries, including theological education, exist to serve the mission of God, not merely to train clergy for the church. Therefore, theological education is an aspect of the church's missionary dimension and expression, and its goal is the transformation of the world. Without suggesting that we adopt his model fully, Banks' missional model could potentially provide a better paradigm for contextual theological education in Asia:

> *The missional model of theological education places the main emphasis on theological mission, on hands-on partnership in ministry based on interpreting the tradition and reflecting on practice with a strong spiritual and communal dimension (Banks 1999, 144).*[8]

The missional model, Banks argues, not only yields a richer integration between theory and practice, moving theological conversations beyond the confines of ecclesiastical concerns, but it also offers different (mission) approaches, methodologies, and attitudes. Such a theology, however, must take the role of the church as God's instrument for mission seriously, and theological education should not be separated from the life and mission of the church (Laing 2009, 41-72). This is not merely a curriculum issue, but a more fundamental structural problem relating to the whole ideology and presuppositions of theological education. Therefore, theological schools offering mission degrees and programmes will need to dialogue with, and respond to, these important critiques, especially if they are serious about training students for effective ministry in mission contexts.

IMPLICATIONS FOR FORMAL AND NON-FORMAL MODELS

Thus far, our survey of debates on theological aims has highlighted potential problems with delivering mission training, especially in academic settings. Within the limited scope of this chapter, we will reflect on the challenges of integrating mission training in the context of formal and non formal educational settings. Formal programmes are highly structured, largely classroom based, mostly theoretical, and tend towards accreditation. Non formal programmes of training tend towards personal or group study, internship, in-service learning in context, and field-based learning. The faculty's primary role is in mentoring, with graduation not necessarily in passing academic grades (Taylor 1991, 2-12). Each model has its strengths and limitations, and complementary roles for training. Between these two models, there are many other mediating and creative models such as theological education by extension, internet based cohorts, apprenticeship in the mission community, field base training, which combine academic research with practice.

Having taught in a formal educational setting in Britain, I recognise that there are many advantages offered by mission training centres in Western countries and believe there is a continuing role for such centres for training, especially for those engaging in postgraduate research. Among key advantages offered are: 1) established theories of teaching and learning 2) training for critical thinking 3) diversity of student body from four continents[9] and 4) more adequate library resources covering history, theology and literature in mission training.[10] However, there are weaknesses which British based training centres need to overcome. Crucially, some Western institutions may unconsciously adopt the enlightenment assumptions of Western theologies as Christian, progressive, normative and to be universally applied. Also not many students can be trained outside their countries, and there are now many good centres of training regionally. Therefore, our attention will be on centres of training in Asia.

FORMAL MISSION TRAINING PROGRAMMES IN ASIA
To a degree, Asian theological schools are aware of the theological critiques just mentioned,[11] and various attempts have been made to integrate missiology within theological curriculums.[12] Nevertheless, because schools have adopted the structure and ethos of formal education, the following section discusses in greater detail major hurdles to be addressed and overcome in order to bring about mission integration in theological schools.

The challenge of formal education
Our survey indicates that classical structures of theological studies are fairly rigid and not so easily reformed so as to integrate different mission goals and priorities. Firstly, the goals of academic learning in biblical studies and theological studies are inclined to focus extensively on intellectual domains, and are normally evaluated through examinations and grading of academic papers. Faculty and leadership of these schools may be led by administrators and academicians who may have little experience in or exposure to the global mission expansion of Christianity.

Secondly, students enrolled into the specialisations of Systematic theology, Old Testament or New Testament departments could graduate with limited ability to connect their specialisations in biblical and systematic theology, church history, or even practical theology, to the concerns and goals of the church's role in society.

Thirdly, in denominational schools, it is sometimes easier to maintain and strengthen accumulated patterns of traditional education than learning approaches which destabilise the status quo with new contextual questions arising from surrounding societies (Rooy 1988, 51-72).[13]

The fourth challenge relates to the need to broaden the focus of theological education from ordained, clergy training for the training for the laity for mission. Mission education must extend to equip lay

7

leadership to serve in diverse areas of public life and vocations in the world. Sometimes, gifted lay leaders may not be able to access traditional full time theological education, but contextual training will need to be made accessible to these lay leaders.

Finally, many academic centres continue to struggle with their extensive focus on information download rather than formation of character. Good training is not just a matter of the mind, but also *poesis*, (matters of the heart and being), as asserted by Stackhouse: 'Symbols not only touch the mind and its conceptions, and evoke action with a purpose, but compel the heart. Perhaps the neglect of symbol is what makes so much of academic ethics and social action so boring' (Stackhouse 1988, 104).

The challenge of contextualisation

All theology is contextual, and the Christian gospel is mediated through embedded cultures. Hence the gospel message, in order to be understood, has to be communicated in ways that are culturally relevant and meaningful (Bevans 2009, 52-53). We need to challenge Christians to understand the context they live in, especially the contemporary culture, in order to understand themselves better and to live out God's missional imperatives (Ingleby 2011, 41-97). Although located in a specified local and mission contexts, it is possible that curriculum content, teaching methodologies and syllabi in Asian theological schools may not always reflect the needs and challenges of Asian societies.

> *...despite all efforts on contextualization some theological seminaries in the regions of the South, especially those who are using English as a medium of instruction, in the post-independent era have become a kind of elite institution producing local leaders for the management of church structures and institutions maintaining "status quo", instead of continuing to create mission impulses in the community and benefiting the whole people of God in a specific context.*[14]

Non contextualised approaches are defined as studies which are developed in one context and being taught to students without undergoing the processes of de-contextualisation from its original setting and re-contextualisation into the student's contexts of ministries. The danger of non contextualisation is that underlying worldviews are not being addressed, resulting in superficial Christianity.[15] When a student's formative education, tutors, subject of studies, heroes, histories, theologians are mostly mediated through dominant (normally Western) traditions, the omitted aspect of learning for whatever good reasons is perceived as having less value or as unimportant. For example, crucial issues such as beliefs in the spirit world, hospitality, ancestor veneration, conversion from hybrid identities, suffering and witnessing as minority communities, may not be covered adequately in Western curriculums. Subjects such as 'unjust social structures of society' and 'creation care' could be other examples which are often omitted from the curriculum due to the complexity of such issues. It is easier to give a cursory coverage through theological ideas rather than confronting those issues within a particular context of learning.

These challenges are not insurmountable but represent issues which need to be reflected upon and addressed theologically and structurally, so that 'mission departments' within these academic centres could serve as 'a gadfly in the house of theology'.

> *Missiology acts as a gadfly in the house of theology, creating unrest and resisting complacency, opposing every ecclesiastical impulse to self-preservation, every desire to stay where we are, every inclination toward provincialism and parochialism, every fragmentation of humanity into regional or sectional blocs . . . . Missiology's task, furthermore, is critically to accompany the missionary enterprise, to scrutinize its foundations, its aims, attitude, message and methods – not from the safe distance of an onlooker, but in a spirit of co-responsibility and service to the church of Christ (Bosch 1991, 496).*

NON-FORMAL MISSION TRAINING PROGRAMMES IN ASIA

The rapid growth of mission movements in Asia has resulted in the growth of mission training programmes in Asia (Harley 1995, 6-7). As indicated earlier, these could be 'in-house mission training programmes' offered by churches, mission agencies or short term training programmes.

The contributions from missiology

Although non formal training centres in Asia have many advantages, there are some major challenges faced by these training centres. Leaders of these training centres often need support in library resources, funding for faculty development, and long term partnership, especially to design mission oriented training programmes. Many of these leaders recognise that a major weakness in short term and practical training schools is their lack of engagement with good missiology. In the last fifty years, missiology has developed as a separate discipline, with its own body of literature, professional guilds, journals, and theologians. Mission study centres in Asia would benefit from engagement with these mission thinkers and their research traditions of missiology.[16] The availability of online mission journals such as the International Bulletin for Missionary Research and International Journal of Frontiers Mission has made mission research more accessible.[17]

Having access to mission studies does not necessarily translate into good training. The greater need is for good training whereby students are acquainted and able to do theology through 'missiological tools' and 'frameworks of reference,' that correlate to grassroot mission reflections. After a time of reflective practice, new and creative paradigms for mission engagements could be promoted. There are advantages for accreditation by bodies which would help to maintain standards and recognition of this non-formal training. However, this need for accreditation can only be meaningfully undertaken if accrediting authorities themselves are self-critical of the problems with theological education, and its own lack of missional orientations.

The call for contextualisation

In order to analyse and understand contexts, one will need to benefit from sociological approaches, including engaging in contextual field research. Observation of religious practices and theoretical analyses must sit alongside the study of Christian theology and biblical studies. Thus, theological education that is contextual and global should equip students with multiple opportunities to study, observe and analyse in the threefold exercise of: 1) exploring the religious thought of one or more traditions so as to understand each in its integrity and diversity, and to grasp its integrative role in relation to the beliefs, and practices of individual faith communities, 2) analysing the historical, cultural, social and political world in which these religious communities function, and 3) developing a distinctive Evangelical Christian position or critique in the midst of multi-faiths and their diverse and contextual perspectives. Contextual Theological Studies used to be viewed as dialogue with cultures and world religions. In addition, Asian Theological

Studies will also need to draw from other disciplines, for example, Regional Studies, such as South East Asia Studies; Cultural Studies, such as Malay, Chinese, Indian Civilisation Studies; Religious Studies, such as Islam, Buddhism, Hinduism as socio-religious communities; and Asian Philosophies, including how these have negotiated new identities in a modern world.

To be effective in a cross cultural situation, the student will need to learn 1) self-awareness of his or her own personality and cultural limitations, and 2) how to have a genuine interest in living and learning in community, 3) skills for relating and loving people of different cultures. Mission training offered at grassroots and local levels in Asia could offer as good training, if not better, when compared to established centres in the West, particularly by adding holistic growth in character development, relational and community skills and cross cultural competencies.

However, smaller centres of training may not have the level of expertise found in formal centres of learning. For example, the need to equip churches to respond to the challenges and complexity of religious pluralism would require a certain level of deeper study and understanding of other faiths with sensitivity and scholarship. If our aim is to train students to be 'missiologists in residence' for 'cosmopolitan apologetics', then the focus, apart from personal discipleship, is to take up the challenge to develop contextual frameworks. Fundamentally, our task in non-formal settings is to provide students with the necessary tools to think critically about the larger contexts of mission engagements, to develop mature theological analysis of complex and new situations, especially in theological understanding of another religious and socio-political worldview. Taking mission context seriously requires the reading of the Bible that goes hand in hand with the reading of contemporary cultures and religious histories and philosophies of Asian societies. Contextual theology should include a dialogue between the Christian gospel with local cultures, with people of other faiths, as well as with situations of injustice and oppression (Bevans and Schroeder 2011, 62).

In the same way that Christians cannot do theology that is non contextual, so Christians cannot engage in mission that is not contextual. The way we live as Christians–which is to live in mission–is constantly to live in dialogue with, and discerning our context, and correlating that context with the broader and older Christian tradition (Bevans and Schroeder 2011, 63).

SOME PROPOSALS FOR COLLABORATION

We suggest that some of the challenges highlighted could be addressed together by training institutions, local churches and the larger global community of concerned Christians. What can concerned Christians do to journey and support these goals of mission integration? A possible shared vision is to gather a relational network of friends whose focused aim is to promote a movement of leaders or missiologists in residence in Asia, whereby resources (people, ideas, networks) are aimed at enabling a theological perception of reality that is qualitatively different from that provided by those predecessors and missionaries who have not undergone contextual mission training. Asia needs a variety of training provisions, and training for all kinds of mission engagements. Below are some suggestions:

SPECIALIST MISSION TRAINING PROGRAMMES

In each country, it would be good to facilitate conversations and trust between training centres, local churches and mission bodies to co-operate on training outcomes and shared projects. This is to avoid unnecessary duplication and waste of limited resources. It will also ensure that perspectives of academic, ecclesiastical and mission bodies are brought together for common goals of training. Where appropriate, it is vital to encourage delivery of good mission training programmes which are led by national mission leaders and supported by experienced global mission faculty and infrastructures (curriculum, learning methodologies and literature resources).

The Global Missionary Training Centre in South Korea and the Asian Cross Cultural Training Institute in Singapore are examples of specialist mission training centres which supplement the role of academic institutions in mission training. These centres make mission their integrative motif for existence and purpose. Over the longer term, as more and more Asians serve cross culturally, there will be a need for such specialist mission training centres that act as a hub for mission training. Such specialist training centres will complement existing mission programmes in theological schools in the following distinctive ways:

1. Biblical and theological training where mission is the heart of the training ethos and which focus on wholistic mission, including frontiers of creation and globalisation
2. Interdenominational partnerships between churches, mission agencies, and seminaries (not identified with a single denomination or group)
3. Leadership provided by qualified and experienced trainers and field missionaries
4. Stronger emphasis on spirituality, character formation and cross cultural skills (not just academic modules or general ministerial training)
5. Multicultural and residential community based learning
6. Cultivated relationships with regional training communities, and a contribution towards the mission of the Global church.

Examples of training programmes/activities are: One-year Residential; Short Courses (e.g. 3-6 weeks); Evening Classes; Pre-field missionary preparation – classroom (lectures, seminars, small group discussions) and field based practical experience; Refresher and Renewal Courses for missionary returnees on home assignment; Mission Leaders and Member Care Forum; Research and publication on contextual issues faced by Asian missionaries; and online mission resources and mission community living.

A REGIONAL NETWORK FOR CENTRES OF MISSION TRAINING

As national centres for mission training are developed, Asian leaders of such centres would benefit most if there is a regular forum to exchange ideas and resources with other leaders in a regional (rather than global) network. For example, issues faced in South Asian contexts could be quite different from East Asians contexts. Funding might be a problem but small beginnings could develop through Facebook, social networking, and making use of other regional consultations. A regional network needs to be well planned and coordinated in order to contribute effectively to the vision of contextual training.

Currently, a major part of theological and funding resources continues to reside in the North while the greatest need for imaginative and creative theological developments would be among newer centres of Christianity. A priority on training local leadership, and building capacity for the training of local mission pioneers would be a more strategic use of limited resources.

GLOBAL MISSION FACULTY FOR ASIA

Each year, many mission trainers may visit other training centres to teach, research and learn about mission situations. Instead of uncoordinated individual trips, a secretariat may be able to coordinate these globetrotters for better service. The focus would be not just for trainers to teach their specialisms but to build capacity for a 'mission department' within each partner institution and to find ways in which good tools of missiology could be made accessible to grassroot mission leaders. Through information technology, sharing of expertise and relationships can be sustained after such visits, but only if there is a coordinating body to follow up and manage agreed outcomes. The interdisciplinary nature of missiology requires diverse disciplines and specialisations, which local institutions usually cannot resource. For this reason they would benefit if a consortium of global faculty was willing to pool their resources. Ideally, the movement of faculty would not only be from the West to Asia, but would also consist of a gathering together of a good community of Asian missiologists and trainers, to support them and to invite their contributions to the church globally, in Africa, Latin America as well as to the Western world.

CONCLUDING REFLECTIONS

My argument is not so much that we need to change specific structures or traditions of theological education. God will continue to use a variety of training provisions for His purposes in mission among the nations. Regardless of the mode of training, there is a 'Macedonian call' for more effective contextual and mission paradigms which would strengthen both formal and non formal modes of training in Asia. Good 'contextual mission training' would ideally reflect the following marks: 1) a theological recovery of the role of the whole church as participants in God's mission (*Missio Dei* and Trinitarian Theology); 2) an undergirding theological *telos* that is missional, 3) missiologically informed 'interpretive tools and frameworks' which take the student's ministry contexts seriously, and 4) a movement of 'missiologists-in-residence' skilful in 'cosmopolitan apologetics'. This vision for contextual mission training in Asia is not just the call for a few more theologians; rather we have a critical need for a movement of prophetic mission to engage with Asian societies meaningfully and effectively. I end this chapter with the prayer from Archbishop Oscar Romero, martyred on 24th March 1980:

> *We cannot do everything, and there is a sense of liberation in realising that.*
> *This enables us to do something, and to do it very well.*
> *It may be incomplete, but it is a beginning, a step along the way,*
> *An opportunity for God's grace to enter and do the rest.*
> *We may never see the end results, but that is the difference*
> *Between the Master builder and the worker. We are workers not master builders,*
> *Ministers, not messiahs. We are prophets of a future not our own.*[18]

THE HERMENEUTICAL PRINCIPLE IN RELATION TO CONTEXTUAL MISSION TRAINING

JONATHAN INGLEBY

Jonathan Ingleby was formerly head of mission studies, Redcliffe College, Gloucester, UK.

One of the questions that any theology must ask is 'Whose material interest is being served?' As Marsha Hewitt says, 'A theology that disregards this question accommodates itself, consciously or not, to the social conditions in which it is contextualised' (2004, 455). The word which caught my eye in this sentence was 'contextualised'. As Stephen Bevans famously said, 'There is no such thing as "theology"; there is only *contextual* theology' (2010, 3). The idea that we can take *our* (let us say, for the sake of argument, Western theology emanating from Western churches and academies) theology, and pretend that it is not *already* contextualised in a complex web of 'social conditions' is an illusion. What we have to determine is: what material interests is *my* theology serving and how openly is this acknowledged?

In asking this question we need to remember that essentially this is a matter of power relations. The representatives of the West, whether statesmen, or soldiers, or educators, or missionaries have always represented their truth as normative – the standard against which others are to be judged. In doing this they have failed to acknowledge that their theology (or if they do not believe in God, their version of the truth) is also a contextual theology, something which puts it on a par with all other contextual theologies – and there are no other sorts of theology, as we have already said. This failure to start with an equality, was and is, an exercise in power. If I can claim that my truth is normative, then I can also claim that I have the right to decide.

My suggestion here is that we look first of all, not at the theology itself (i.e. by asking whether it is sound, or evangelical or systematic), but at other people's 'social conditions'. As the saying goes, 'the *critical* hermeneutical principle is the context'. This would mean that when it comes to *method* the Liberation Theology people have it right. As they might put it: 'Given the material conditions under which our people are suffering, what sort of theology (and therefore theological education) is required so that it might be a truly contextual theology?'

I can easily imagine the objections to this. What about the danger of a contextualisation which is unfaithful to the authentic gospel? Did not the Paul who wanted to be 'all things to all people' for the sake of the gospel, also warn us about preaching 'another gospel' which was not true to the message which he had originally delivered?

Let me give two Biblical illustrations of what I have in mind. It seems likely that the faith of Israel when it first encountered the inhabitants of Canaan, did not feel it necessary to oppose the culture, even the religious culture, that it confronted. The founding father, Abraham, and his immediate descendants, at least as described in the book of Genesis, were happy enough with sacred trees and places, with local sites for the construction of altars and with other similar religious practices, even when these had been previously established by the Canaanite population. (Genesis 12:6, 13:18, 21:33). Abraham also adopted the chief Canaanite title for God without apparent embarrassment. (We can compare Genesis 14, 19-20 with 14:22; in the latter reference Abraham combines the local name El Elyon and his own preferred name for God, Yahweh.)[19] Claus Westermann, in his commentary on Genesis says that 'there is not so much as a single reference [in Genesis] which rejects Canaanite religion or morality' (Westermann 1985 cited in Brett 2009, 52 n. 22).[20] In some ways, this rather gentle and accommodating approach continued during and after the conquest, though there was never any question of condoning disloyalty to Yahweh (e.g. Joshua 24:25-6, I Samuel 9:12-14). At a later time it was thought necessary to change tactics; the permissiveness with regard to local sites of worship became particularly unacceptable. A huge effort was made to centralise Yahwism in Jerusalem, for example. Kings like Hezekiah and Josiah were prominent in this sort of political action. They were not necessarily wrong, of course, but we need to understand what was happening. It reminds us of the point made above that in matters of culture and religion the power equation almost inevitably comes into play.

The lesson for today may well be twofold. Firstly that we need to go very gently – I had almost said courteously – in approaching another culture, happy in many instances to take our example from Abraham. Abraham's approach was to come alongside, to use what he could find locally, to incorporate rather than exclude, to deal with the familiar – and to be loyal to Yahweh. Secondly, we need to be careful not to allow the power agenda to *dictate* our contextualisation. In the end we may have no choice about this, but we need to be aware of the way that issues of power and control distort what we are trying to do.

A second example might be the way that the early Christian church coped with the influx of Gentile believers. There is no doubt that the apostles and other church leaders struggled with the idea of a change in religious practice. Peter, on the occasion of his famous visit to the house of Cornelius is concerned with the implications of eating a meal in a Gentile home (Acts 10:28). His vision in Joppa, just previous to this, had troubled him precisely because it commanded him to do something which was forbidden in the ritual law (Acts 10: 14). At the Council of Jerusalem there was divided opinion among the Jewish believers about how to receive Gentile converts. What would be their relationship, once converted, to the whole Jewish legal apparatus? One party maintained that Gentiles must be circumcised and told to keep the Law of Moses (Acts 15:5). However, according to Peter, this entailed the converts carrying 'a yoke which neither we nor our forefathers were able to bear' (Acts 15: 10).

I wonder whether we can easily imagine what a change of attitude and approach this new way of thinking required of the devout Jews in the audience. Hitherto, what might be called 'religious power' was deemed to be theirs. They had, by virtue of physical descent and adherence to the *torah*, the position of privilege. It might be possible for Gentiles to enjoy some of these advantages, but only if they, the outsiders, accepted and practised the rules of the insiders. Now, there was a level playing field. 'For our belief', says Peter, 'is that we [Jews] are saved in the same way as they [Gentiles] are: by the grace of the Lord Jesus' (Acts 15:11). Indeed, in some ways, the playing field is tilted in favour of the Gentiles. In most cases Gentiles would have had little difficulty (in terms of religion, anyway) in sitting down and sharing a meal with Jews. But Jewish people – certainly the more pious ones – would have found the reverse very difficult. This was still a big issue among Jewish believers when Paul wrote to the Galatians some years later (Galatians 2:11-12). The so-called decree of the Jerusalem council (Acts 15: Acts 15:28-29) which did lay down some 'rules' for Gentile admission to Christian fellowship seems to have been largely about giving up attendance at idol feasts (Witherington

III 1998, 460-7). It is true that this comes up as an issue in Paul's correspondence (1 Corinthians 8:1-13, 10:14-32) and may have been more difficult for Gentiles than we sometimes realise because attendance at these feasts was socially important. It seems likely, nevertheless, that the early church had more trouble instructing its Jewish than its Gentile members about breaking down the 'dividing wall' between the two communities. This was because the changes demanded of Jewish Christians, even when they were the majority, were very profound. They had, in due course, to leave temple and synagogue, to abandon their food laws and exclusive dining rules, to cease to claim privilege on account of their natural ancestry (see Philippians 3:5) and to enter into a new equality (Galatians 3:28).

My point is this. It was, in religious terms, the dominant and powerful religious culture that had to give way in order that others might be introduced to the gospel. This was exceptional. It was true of the early church but since then it has hardly ever been the case, certainly from the time of Constantine. Even when the Christian faith was introduced by those who were apparently politically weaker, as in some aspects of the modern missionary movement, they took the religious and cultural higher ground, founding churches in their own image and expecting the newly initiated to join them on their terms.

The lesson here is that we may need to *create* situations in which other people's social conditions are more powerful than ours. I am thinking again of those people to whom we are ministering the gospel. This, it seems to me, is what Paul was speaking about when he claimed to be 'all things to all people'. Paul's apostolic record was one of service and suffering. He meant it when he said that he had stepped down from the place of privilege (Philippians 3:4-11). Paul's gospel was contextualised in his own weakness so that he could be aware of the context of others and respond to it. He kept on giving away his own power, so that he might empower others.

Our normal description of contextualisation begins with matters such as language learning and culture. If what I say about contextualisation is true, however, then contextualisation may be more a matter of power structures. I was struck by the observation of an anthropologist writing about Bible translation work, who commented that 'indigenising' projects [such as Bible translation] are often elitist attempts, imposed from top down, to control the direction of religious synthesis' (Stewart and Shaw 1994, 12). Here I cannot help thinking about the Machiguengas, the tribal group so brilliantly described in Mario Vargas Llosa's novel *The Storyteller* (1990).[21] The hero in the story, Saul Zuratas, is not a tribal himself, indeed he is a Peruvian half-Jew, but is accepted by the Machiguengas because he has learned the skill of re-telling to the people the stories that crucially make up their identity. Zuratas is not a Christian missionary, far from it, but for a Christian the question might be how one might emulate him if called to be 'an apostle to the Machiguengas'. In the story, the gospel has already arrived, through the medium of some dedicated Bible translators. These, however, are intent upon conveying their message by means of *changing* the Machiguengas' culture. They are gathering them into villages and 'educating' them, so that they might read the Bible when it is translated. Is this not precisely yet one more example of 'elitist attempts, imposed from top down, to control the direction of religious synthesis'?

It is worth noting that in the debate about the nature of 'syncretism' on the whole missionaries have given the word a meaning – believing two contradictory truths at the same time – which is some distance from its original meaning. Apparently the English word derives from a Greek term denoting 'a combination of Cretans'; the Cretans were famous, in the ancient world, for quarrelling among themselves but uniting against a common enemy (Stewart and Shaw 1994, 3). Perhaps the 'insider movements' such as the Muslim Background Believers in Bangladesh, could indeed be described as 'syncretic' in this more generous way. In a context where, for example, both Christians and Muslims consider 'insider Christians' to be in error, they are united against this condemnatory opinion by becoming syncretists (good sense): followers of Jesus within a Muslim culture. My point here is that these people have the right to represent themselves, and that this right is part of the power equation, which often comes down to how we define certain words.

In mission we have found this requirement to treat others as equals, not to put ourselves as *Christians* above others, to be particularly challenging. We are frightened of what others might say about us, particularly the accusation that we have given in to theological relativism or syncretism, and are hoping that whatever happens we may retain our *theological* dominance. Often we do not even want to talk about this. We earnestly desire relationship but are uncomfortable with the inevitable change that this brings.

So, if we are truly committed to a *contextualised* mission training, how are we to proceed, particularly within the Asian context? I go to conferences, read reviews and articles, confer with mission leaders. There is a sort of ideological conflict going on between a systematised and traditional theology on the one hand and the difficult business of contextualisation on the other. Again and again what strikes me is that traditionalists display an attitude of suspicion which derives from the desire to be in control backed by an Enlightenment rather than a Biblical world-view. We are like the man in the parable who buries his precious talent in the ground and refuses to put it into circulation. It is precisely the moment when we are required to hand over our version of the truth to the context that we find difficult. Can we not start again and envisage a truly contextualised Asian missionary training informed by a contextualised theology and praxis? It is dispiriting that so often our idea of contextualisation means little more than listing Asian characteristics and values (Asians are more family oriented, more respectful of elders, less individualistic and so on) but misses out on the big challenges: vulnerability, kenosis, suffering, risk, even a measure of uncertainty and disorientation.

So let me suggest some basic working principles.

NO CONTEXTUALISATION WITHOUT CONSTRUCTION

Mission training, particularly in Asia, will need to take on board that theology will need to be *constructed* in order to match particular contexts. I like the illustration (Hodgson 1994 cited in Sørensen 2007, 216) of theology being navigation which responds to, but does not produce or control, the weather. Are we training people to be navigators, to be interpreters rather than legislators, to use Zygmunt Bauman's well-known distinction (1992, 1-25)? How is this done? David Harley (this volume) speaks of flexibility. Tan Kang San (this volume) writes of 'learning approaches which destabilise the status quo with new contextual questions arising from surrounding societies.'

I think this point about construction is the most fundamental, and difficult, point I want to make. We tend to think of the gospel as a package which we need to deliver faithfully to the recipient, though we agree that the wrapping paper may be different in different contexts. The package itself, however, is certain, changeless and perfect. The trouble is that all knowledge is to some extent an enterprise of human construction – and that includes my knowledge of the gospel, and the way that others get to know it too. Because the knower helps to constitute what is known, the context, i.e. the socio-economic and political reality of the knower, is decisive for knowledge. When we engage in Christian proclamation, therefore, we are inviting the hearer to imagine, or *construct,* a new world (Brueggemann 1993, 17-18). But people necessarily do this by building together the pieces of their 'given' world-view which remain useful to them, and the pieces (not a full-grown system which would be another form of imperialism) that are now provided for them as new construction materials. (This is sometimes called *bricolage,* the formation of fresh cultural forms from the ready-to-hand debris of the old ones.) For the proclamation to be effective (and effectively contextualised) the construction work must be done by the hearer.[22]

NO CONSTRUCTION WITHOUT CONVERSATION

The way in which people are helped to construct their new world is through conversation (Brueggemann 1993, 10). My Christian faith is practised from a given perspective which I have preferred to other perspectives. In conversation with others I may advocate this perspective but I must also listen to theirs – otherwise it is not a conversation. I have to admit, of course, that my perspective is only one possible way to look at things. I also think that the conversation should be as much about how those involved are going to build their lives together, as about establishing 'the truth'. In conversation we should be aiming at what Richard Rorty describes as 'an expanding repertoire of alternative descriptions rather than The One Right Description' (Gergen 1999, 168), remembering that context is always local and therefore plural.

NO CONVERSATION WITHOUT RELATIONSHIP

Imagining a world together demands mutual trust, perhaps even friendship. The conversation partners must be committed to each other. As already said, relationship to be worth anything, must incorporate the possibility of change. 'Transformative dialogue' is one description of this. Because change is threatening, the relationship must be one of trust. Westerners must be particularly careful about this. The Enlightenment Project has always had an air of anxiety about it, something which has led to a desire to control others because we are not sure that we can trust them. Much of our defective contextualisation, conversation and relationship stems from an unwillingness to give away our power.

So what should our mission training be like? What I write in conclusion should, I think, be true for all mission training, but I believe it is particularly relevant in the Asian context because of the relative failure of the gospel to be 'heard' among the great world religions there, and because the context is so various.

We Westerners have been exceedingly cautious, even timid, in our practise of contextualisation. We have domesticated the gospel, or what we conceive to be the gospel, 'to accommodate regnant modes of knowledge and to enhance regnant modes of power' (Brueggemann 1993, 7) – a good description of the ever-present danger of imperialistic attitudes. By contrast, Asian missionaries need to throw themselves into the market place of ideas and commit themselves to 'the persuasive advocacy and adjudication of competing construals, perspectives and paradigms of reality' (Brueggemann 1993, 12). Truth is like the manna in the wilderness. It cannot be hoarded and remain fresh. It must be put into circulation.

How can we educate people to be vulnerable? If we teach them to hide behind theological absolutes, perhaps expressed as a systematic theology, we cannot go forward. Once we admit that knowledge is local, particular, plural, timely (as against timeless) then there is a huge amount of learning to be done. I think that this also applies to the way that we teach and learn the Bible. The world is made up of 'little' people with 'small' contextualised stories, specific to them and their circumstances. But it is stories of this sort that we find in the Bible. Yet we read the Bible as if it had only *one* story (Brueggemann 1993, 69-70).

There are practical things that we can do about this. We can educate our theologians and missiologists to understand the world better. They can be taught to pay attention to local knowledge, to appreciate the plural nature of their contexts, to be alert to timely truth. When planning missionary training it should not be just a matter of theology, philosophy and history, but also sociology, economics, politics, geography, culture studies, media studies, anthropology and of course religions. (See Tan Kang San in this volume.) At the same time we can teach the Bible better.

It is still true that Scripture provides the way pre-eminently by which we faithfully imagine and construct our world. But do we teach Scripture with this in mind?

All of the above, if it is to be done well, will demand much time. I suspect there are no short cuts when it comes to good missionary training. Also, institutions will be necessary: colleges, courses, means of administration, structures and schedules, appropriate buildings and technology, these must all be designed to serve the missionary community, without overpowering or exploiting it.

A huge task lies before us. It is one which will require courage, imagination, endeavour, patience and skill. All the more reason for getting on with it.

HERE BE DRAGONS – SOME GUIDELINES FOR EXPLORERS IN CONTEXTUAL MISSION AND THEOLOGY IN ASIA

DAVID MILLER

David Miller served for ten years in Japan with OMF International, working mainly in student ministry. After returning to Scotland, he began teaching at International Christian College in Glasgow, where he lectures in mission studies.

'Here be dragons'. This ominous phrase has come to signify the presence of the unknown, to alert travellers to the perils of venturing into unexplored and potentially dangerous places. Interestingly, despite the fact that the phrase is widely known, there is today only one surviving example of its actual use, and that is on the Hunt-Lenox globe, dating from the early 16th century. Perhaps significantly, it is used there to refer to the east coast of Asia, so it seemed an appropriate title and metaphor for what this chapter attempts to do.

Explorers were torn between the desire to get to know the unknown lands before them, with all their promise and potential, and an awareness of the dangers which might lie in wait. They would have to take risks, but without taking sensible precautions, then they would not return safely. In mission in Asia today the tension between on the one hand the desire to explore and find new and perhaps more appropriate ways of engaging in mission and building for the kingdom and on the other the dangers of not staying true to the Gospel is keenly felt, including by many of the contributors to this book. How can those who engage in mission, both national Christians and those who cross cultures to work alongside them or as pioneers where there is no church, open up new possibilities for faithful mission, while avoiding the 'dragons' - of syncretism, or of heresy, or conversely of being guilty of importing an alien form of Christianity which will not flourish in its new setting?

This tension in Asian mission is almost as old as the Hunt-Lenox globe itself. In the 16th century the Jesuits in Japan took their first tentative steps towards a contextualised approach to mission under

Alessandro Valignano, resulting in criticisms from other missionary orders such as the Franciscans. In the 17th century Matteo Ricci inaugurated a more radical and controversial approach to contextualisation in China, resulting in the order being accused of syncretism in the Rites controversy which came to a head in the 18th century.[23] Nor should we underestimate the shock caused among the missionary community in China in the 19th century by Hudson Taylor as he sought to identify with the Chinese people by dressing like them rather than retaining his Western dress. The 20th century and the early years of the 21st have seen the emergence of many different approaches to mission and of local contextual theologies across Asia, a few of which are explored in this volume.[24] Yet despite, or perhaps because of, this long history, the search for authentic patterns of contextualisation in Asian mission continues.

This is partly because as contexts change, so the expression of the Gospel will also change, meaning that one can never claim to have arrived at a definitive pattern of contextualisation. This is particularly the case in Asia, a continent which has experienced dramatic changes over the preceding centuries. It is also culturally, religiously and economically very diverse which arguably makes the challenge of authentic contextualisation more acute. However, it may also be because of the lingering suspicion that somehow we are not getting it right in Asia. Sub-Saharan Africa and Latin America have been characterised by significant Christian growth but not so in Asia. Even where growth has been notable, in South Korea, among segments of the population of India, and in China, Christianity remains a minority presence, and many cultures appear to be resistant to the claims of Christ.

This apparent lack of response raises questions among many cross-cultural workers in Asia. I suspect that those engaged in mission tend to be activist by personality, frequently moved by a sense of the urgency of the Gospel and a passion especially for those who have not had the chance to respond to the claims of Christ. This activism and passion rightly drives them to search for approaches to mission which may appear to offer greater impact, and at the same time may make them critical of those approaches which do not appear to be as effective. Such people are those who push at the boundaries – in other words, they are the explorers who venture into the areas where the 'dragons' may be encountered.

So, if there are no maps to guide us as we embark on new and risky ventures in contextual mission, are there other resources which may help us to navigate this complex landscape? I want to suggest that there are certain principles which should help us weigh up any new approaches which may be considered. These are not so much hard and fast tests to ensure theological and missiological 'soundness' but rather pointers to areas of possible danger, or to safer routes forward. If we continue with the metaphor of exploration, we might liken them to lighthouses, which do not tell sailors exactly where to go, but do warn of dangerous reefs to be avoided.

These foundational principles are ones which have been identified by Professor Andrew Walls and to which he draws attention in his seminal essay 'The Gospel as Prisoner and Liberator of Culture' (Walls, 1996: 3 - 15). Here Walls surveys the history of Christian expansion, noting both the great differences in form and expression which Christianity has taken as it has crossed from one culture into another and made itself at home and also its continuities, those elements of the Gospel which are constant over time. As continuities he counts the person of Christ, Scripture and the sacraments, as well as the shared consciousness of being part of the same people of God despite all the differences. He identifies two fundamental tensions which Christians face in any situation where they seek to be faithful to Christ as well as to their context. The first of these tensions is between what he calls the indigenising principle and the pilgrim principle. The second is the tension between the particular local expression of the Gospel and the universalising factor of membership of the people of God. Recognising the importance, not just of the individual principles but of the inevitable tension between them seems to me to be crucial in engaging in authentic contextual mission.

Writing of the indigenising principle he says 'It is of the essence of the Gospel that God accepts us we are... In Christ God accepts us together with our group relations; with that cultural conditioning that makes us feel at home in one part of human society and less at home in another' (Walls, 1996: 7). It is clear, as both Scripture from the Council of Jerusalem onwards and history affirm, that one can be a Christian in one's own culture, and need not become culturally Jewish (or Greek or British or American). The Gospel can make itself at home in any and every culture. At the heart of what we seek to do in mission then is helping people to become authentic followers of Jesus within their own cultural context, rather than calling them to become 'like us'.

However, Walls goes on to point out that this indigenising principle is in tension with what he calls the pilgrim principle. This 'whispers to [the Christian] that he has no abiding city and warns him that to be faithful to Christ will put him out of step with his society; for that society never existed...which could absorb the word of Christ painlessly into its system' (1996: 8). It is important to grasp this point as it means that a clash with some elements of any culture and resistance to the message of the Gospel is inevitable. Steve Bevans also draws attention to this in his analysis of what he describes as the countercultural model of contextual theology (Bevans, 2008: 117ff). This in turn raises the question 'Can there be degrees of resistance to the Gospel depending on the cultural soil in which the seed is sown?' The metaphor of seed and sowing reminds us of two things. Firstly, it points us to the parable of the sower, where Jesus clearly suggests that his followers may expect different types of response to the Gospel depending on the nature of the soil in which it is sown. Secondly, it echoes the words of the Japanese Christian novelist Endo Shusaku, who puts into the mouth of one of his characters, the apostate Jesuit missionary Ferreira in the novel *Silence*, these oft-quoted words:

> *This country is a swamp. In time you will come to see that for yourself. This country is a more terrible swamp than you can imagine. Whenever you plant a sapling in this swamp the roots begin to rot; the leaves yellow and wither. And we have planted the sapling of Christianity in this swamp (Endō, 1982: 237).*

Although *Silence* is a historical novel set in the early 17th century, Endo is at the same time exploring one of his constant themes, namely the apparent unsuitability of Christianity to the Japanese cultural context in the 20th century. He believes that the problem lies in the nature of Japanese culture, which he characterises as a swamp. He is thus echoing the parable, namely that lack of growth and limited response to the Gospel is not necessarily an indication of poor sowing, in other words of failed or inadequate contextualisation, but may as likely be due to the quality of the cultural 'soil'. A natural response to lack of growth or unresponsiveness to the Gospel will be to feel that there must be a better way, and it is right to explore to see if a better way exists. However, it may also be that, mysteriously, at certain times in particular cultural contexts, however authentic our contextualisation – and it is wiser to talk about authentic rather than effective contextualisation, lest we come to think of contextualisation simply as some kind of technique – this is the nature of the response. Cultural contexts can change, as the Lord of history works out His purposes. There was a time when both Korea and China seemed hard and resistant to the Gospel, yet the faithful sowing of the seed of the Gospel, sometimes in blood, meant that when conditions changed and people began to search for something, there were *local* Christians there ready to point to the One who is the source of life and hope. For those of us who have worked in the apparently resistant areas of Asia, for example in Japan, Thailand, or among Muslim people groups across southeast Asia the challenge is not only to seek more authentic approaches to contextualisation, but also to continue to pray, to wait in hope, and to persevere in sowing and planting, rejoicing in the response which we do see and remembering that ultimately, as Paul reminds us, it is God who gives the increase (1 Cor. 3: 6).

Our first 'lighthouse', then, is the awareness of the continuing tension between the indigenising and the pilgrim principles. The second is being alert to the related tension which Walls also notes that there is between the particular and the universal factors in the expression of the church in any cultural context. When he speaks of 'particular' factors he is in effect expressing in a different way what is inherent in the indigenising principle, the fact that the Gospel can make itself at home in any cultural context. However, when he talks about 'universalising' factors, he is not so much meaning the things which make Christians pilgrims in any society, but the things which mean that Christians in any cultural context are also part of a worldwide family. No expression of Christian faith should be so localised or particular that those Christians are unable to relate to the wider church. It is this 'adoption into Israel' which brings 'Christians of all cultures and ages together through a common inheritance, lest any of us make the Christian faith such a place to feel at home that no one else can live there' (Walls, 1996: 9). In other words, there are things which should unite all Christians of whatever cultural context. This may seem obvious, but when one sets this in the context of striving for authentic contextualisation the tension emerges. The more localised and particular an expression of Christian faith is, the more likely it is to be inaccessible to a Christian from a different context. The sense of discomfort which a psalm-singing Presbyterian from the Highlands of Scotland may well feel on first experience of worship in a black-majority Pentecostal church in inner city London might be one example of this. By definition contextualisation means a striving for localisation. But the universal nature of the Gospel means that those who minister in whatever context must seek to instil in local(-ised) Christians an awareness of the fact that they belong to a worldwide family. There needs to be in the life of the church *now* an anticipation of the vision of people from every race, nation, tribe and language joining in the worship of the lamb (Rev. 7: 9). Part of this will involve a broadening of experience and understanding of what it means to be Christian, which may result on occasions in a sense of strangeness and perhaps even discomfort. However, recognising there are some universals is vital in ensuring that the local expression does not drift into syncretism and remains truly Christian, even if in some ways it puts itself at odds with the surrounding culture. The decision of the Council of Jerusalem that Gentile believers should abstain from food offered to idols meant that they were being commanded to do something which did not sit well within their cultural context, yet it was vital in ensuring that their worship was directed to the one true God, and that there was no compromise with those demonic forces which Paul reminds us lurk behind human attempts to reach the divine (Acts 15: 29; cf. 1 Cor. 10: 20).

So, what might these universals be, and are there things which those who engage in mission in an Asian context need particularly to note? Are those constants which Walls identifies, namely the worship of Jesus, celebration of the sacraments and reverence for the Scriptures, sufficient? Given the challenges inherent in the variety of Asian contexts I would like to suggest that there are at least three universals which those involved in contextualisation in Asia need to remember.

The first concerns the nature of God. To be faithful to both Scripture and tradition, thus ensuring a sense of connectedness to the universal church, we need to understand God as Trinity and as Creator, distinct from creation. In the religiously plural context of Asia, where God may be understood clearly as a unity in which there can be no division, or as one with the universe, or simply as one of an array of deities who must be manipulated and appeased, the understanding of God as He reveals Himself in Jesus and in scripture will inevitably challenge all of these understandings. It is true that Scripture does not explicitly refer to God as 'Trinity', but as Alister McGrath notes 'Scripture bears witness to a God who demands to be understood in a Trinitarian way' (McGrath, 1997: 294).

The second universal to be emphasised in an Asian context is that Jesus must be affirmed as the incarnate Son of God, crucified and risen. Here too this understanding of Jesus will challenge those religious perspectives which see Jesus as a prophet, or as one of many deities, or manifestations of the divine, or indeed as simply a teacher or guru to be rated against teachers in other traditions. He *is* both prophet and teacher, but he is much more and uniquely more than that.

Both of these universals draw on the long theological tradition of the church and are expressed in both the historic creeds. Significantly, McGrath draws a distinction between the creeds and the more specific 'confessions' of particular denominations. 'A "creed" has come to be recognised as a concise, formal and *universally accepted* and authorised statement of the main points of the Christian faith' (1997: 17 – italics mine). True, many of the early theological debates of the church were conducted using the vocabulary of the Greek philosophical tradition. It is inevitable that Christian faith and truth must be expressed in cultural forms, because we have nothing else with which to do it. A recent collection of essays looking at evangelicals and contextual theology explores this (Cook et al, 2010). However, recognising the limitations of cultural forms of expressions of Christian truth is not the same as saying that the truths which they seek to capture are inappropriate or irrelevant for an Asian (or any other non-Western context). Robert Hood, in his book *Must God Remain Greek?* (Hood, 1990), explores this same question in the context of Afro-Caribbean cultures. He argues powerfully for engaging with local religious traditions, concepts and vocabulary in the search for contextually appropriate expressions of theology, yet still recognises the significance of the creeds, referring to them as 'minimum boundaries but not the final limits of Christology'(1990: 152). And what must be remembered is that in appropriating the vocabulary and concepts of local cultures, including the Greek culture of the early centuries of the church, words and concepts are given *transformed* meanings as they become vehicles for expressing the truth of the Gospel, as Benno van den Toren notes. 'In the Trinitarian discussion, the church used terms such as homoousios, hupostasis and ousia which had been used before in other philosophical discourse, but which took on new meanings in order to be able to describe the reality of the Trinity for which hitherto existing language was simply inadequate' (Van den Toren, 2010: 101).

What this means then in terms of contextual mission and theology in an Asian (or any other) context is that all localised expressions of Christian truth need to be ultimately faithful to these core beliefs of the church. That is not to say that these are the only words which we may use to talk about God. Finding the right words, images, metaphors etc. to talk about the Triune God and about Jesus without closing down discussion before it has even begun is part of the challenge of contextual mission. We must seek creative and appropriate ways to express these truths in the variety of Asian cultures in which we engage in mission. However, it is vital that in the ways we talk about God and about Jesus we set seekers and local believers on a trajectory that will eventually lead them to an understanding of God, and of Jesus, *that will not be anything other than that which is captured in the creeds, in the traditions of the universal church, and in Scripture.* It may take a long time to arrive there but, for example, a Muslim follower of Isa al-Masih needs to be on the same road that two millennia ago led a good Second Temple Jew called Thomas, on encountering the risen Jesus before him, to say, 'My Lord and my God' (John 20: 28).

This leads to my third 'universal', which is that following Jesus must involve conversion, a theme which could take up a book in itself. Briefly though, the encounter with Christ which we see in the Gospels and in the apostolic preaching in Acts calls for *metanoia*, a change of mind which is both a turning *from* and a turning *to*. It is this which sets converts on a journey towards a life lived under the lordship of Christ. When the Japanese Christian Uchimura Kanzo famously said 'I love two Js and no third; one is Jesus, and the other is Japan' (Uchimura, 1984[1926]: 53) these were words expressing the resolution of the tension between his Japanese identity and his Christian identity, a resolution which a deeply rooted conversion experience enabled him to attain.[25] Conversion then does not mean a *rejection* of the convert's culture, but rather its *transformation* as he or she reintegrates their cultural identity with their identity as followers of Christ.

Inevitably, a focus on 'lighthouses' and warnings against the risks of going astray will result in a negative tone to this chapter. However, it is important to recognise that a right understanding of the *missio Dei* tells us this – though we may find ourselves in cultural contexts where we can say 'here be dragons', yet we can have confidence that as we join Him in the risky adventure of mission we can also say 'Here is God.'

THE TRAINING OF ASIAN MISSIONARIES

DAVID HARLEY

David Harley was the former General Director of OMF International and Principal of All Nations Christian College. He is presently involved in international preaching and teaching ministry.

THE CASE FOR MISSIONARY TRAINING

The last three decades have witnessed exponential growth in the missionary movement within Asia. The churches of Hong Kong, Taiwan, Indonesia, the Philippines, Malaysia and Singapore have sent out increasing numbers of cross-cultural workers. South Korea has more than 16,000 missionaries serving all over the world. Indian churches are now supporting over 30,000 missionaries, working cross-culturally both within the sub-continent and in other parts of the world.

The churches of Asia, together with the churches of Africa and Latin America, are assuming an ever-increasing role in global evangelism. Although accurate statistics are difficult to discover, it is estimated that more than 50% of the global missionary force today consists of Christians from Asia, Africa, Latin America and the Pacific. Missionaries from these continents are already making a huge impact for the gospel within their own region and beyond. By the grace of God they may also play a key role in the re-evangelisation of Europe.

If these Christians from the majority world are to be successful in their endeavour, it is vital they are trained and prepared for cross-cultural ministry. The negative experience of Latin American missionaries in the 1990s provided a stark warning to those who send out new recruits before they have been adequately prepared and equipped. Hundreds of young men and women from Latin America were sent all over the world as missionaries. They went out full of enthusiasm and with high expectations, but they were unprepared for the problems that lay ahead. They didn't know how to adapt to a different culture. They did not get the response or the converts they expected. They were not prepared for the difficulties and delays they encountered. Many returned with a profound sense of failure and some of the churches that sent them began to question the validity of the missionary movement.

Some Asian Christians argue that Asians do not need cross-cultural training to be missionaries in Asia. Unlike their Caucasian brothers and sisters with their Western traditions and perceptions, Asian missionaries are at home with the customs and values of Asian cultures. They are familiar with the fears and aspirations of Asian society, aware of the importance of the family within Asian society and conscious of the need to respect elders. It is easier for them to identify with the local community, since their looks do not make them stand out as 'foreign devils'. They may even know the language or a closely related one.

All this is true. Asian missionaries working in Asia do have significant advantages over those who come from Western countries. Chinese Singaporeans can more easily fit into China. Indians are the best evangelists in their own country. At the same time, it can also be misleading. There are enormous cultural differences between the countries of Asia; between Pakistan and Singapore, between South Korea and Thailand. The acceptable dress codes for women in Pakistan and Singapore are an obvious example. In Pakistan women need to cover their arms, legs and heads, whereas in Singapore young Chinese may go to church wearing shorts. In one country and even within one city, there are many different cultural worlds. Those who fail to respect these differences can easily cause offence and jeopardise the effectiveness of their ministry, whether they are Asian or Caucasian.

The late Professor J. Herbert Kane warned of the consequences of sending out new missionaries without any '*professional* training in cross-cultural communication; missionary anthropology; history, philosophy, and theology of missions; and the non-Christian religions – to say nothing of crucial issues or area studies' (1992, 176). Surveys conducted by the World Evangelical Alliance have indicated that one of the main reasons for missionary attrition is lack of adequate preparation. They have also shown that those who do at least one year of missionary training stay twice as long on the field as those who do not (Taylor, 1997; Hay, 2007).

The purpose of this paper is to suggest some of essential elements that should be included in a training programme for Asian missionary candidates and to examine how such a programme might be structured and adapted within an Asian context.

THE CONTENT OF A TRAINING PROGRAMME

Biblical and theological foundations

The primary function of missionaries is to proclaim the Word of God (Acts 4:31, 6:4, 6:7, 8:4 etc.). It is obviously important they have good knowledge of that Word. This should include an understanding of the story of salvation, familiarity with the different types of literature within the biblical text, and the ability to communicate biblical truth effectively in the cultural context where they minister.

Missionaries also need to be able to explain the major doctrines of the Christian faith. They need to think how to teach these basic doctrines in another context. If their ministry is going to be among monotheists, they will need to know how to explain the doctrine of the Trinity to those who are monotheists. If they work among Hindus or Buddhists, they will have to show the difference between re-incarnation and biblical teaching on spiritual rebirth. If they are addressing people who regard their ancestors as 'the living dead' they will need to know how to explain texts like 'Abraham was gathered unto his ancestors' (Genesis 25:8).

The apostle Paul strove to communicate effectively to his audience, whether they were Jews, polytheists or Greek philosophers. By using his understanding of their culture, he sought to build bridges to communicate his message effectively. Asian missionaries must work equally hard to understand and appreciate the beliefs and values of the people to whom they go. They need to address the beliefs and concerns of their audience and deal with such issues as the veneration of ancestors, the significance of dreams and the power of spirits. In the words of Dean Flemming, their preaching must be audience-sensitive without being audience driven (2005, 116). That is the starting point for the missionary, but their ultimate objective is to introduce their hearers to the risen Saviour, who alone can meet their deepest needs.

Spiritual life and character

Mission is no place for the faint hearted or the walking wounded. Cross-cultural missionaries must be able to survive spiritually in a lonely or hostile environment. They cannot assume there will be a lively church or a dynamic small group where they can gain weekly encouragement. They may have little fellowship or means of spiritual nourishment. Will they be able to cope? Have they learned to feed themselves from the Word of God?

Throughout the New Testament, there is a strong emphasis on the character of those who preach the gospel and minister within the church. The qualities of an elder or deacon, described in the Pastoral Epistles, focus not on academic ability or ministerial gifts (except the gift of teaching), but on character and the spiritual life. When seven deacons were appointed in Acts 6, they were chosen not because they had great administrative gifts or accounting ability, but because they were full of the Holy Spirit and wisdom.

Some missionary candidates have an exalted view of themselves and what they are going to achieve. They have unrealistic ideas about their gifts and abilities. They need to realize that they may not be the great asset and gift to the church to which they go that they and their congregation had fondly imagined. They need to follow Paul's advice not to think of themselves more highly than they ought, but to see themselves from God's perspective.

In the past Western missionaries often displayed a sense of superiority, but white people are not the only ones who can feel a sense of racial superiority. Asian missionaries who go out with high academic qualifications supported by successful and wealthy churches may assume they are superior to the people to whom they go, and may exhibit their ethnocentricity in things they say and attitudes they adopt.

Students need to understand their own culture and its influence on them. They need to be warned against making the assumption that their cultural way of doing things is normative, and superior to other patterns of behaviour. In addition, they need to be prepared for culture shock and be encouraged to become bi-cultural people, capable of appreciating another culture as much as their own.

Jesus warned his disciples that they must be prepared to suffer in the cause of the gospel. When he sent out seventy disciples he told them: 'I send you out like lambs among wolves' (Luke 10:3). When he spoke to the apostles at the last supper, he made it very clear that they would face opposition and rejection. 'If the world hates you, know that it hated me before it hated you' (John 15:18).

In several Asian countries Christians face opposition and persecution. Pastors are put in prison and churches are burned down. Those who proclaim their faith face both prejudice and discrimination. Asian missionaries must not only be taught how to evangelise and plant churches, they must also be taught how to face opposition and persecution.

Missiological reflection

According to Dr Tai Woong Lee, Director of Global Ministries Study Center, a leading missionary training institute in Korea, a high priority in any missionary training programme is to make sure the trainees have a clear understanding of mission theology. Initially students will study the biblical basis of mission, tracing the biblical vision for the nations of the world from the early chapters of Genesis to the eschatological climax in Revelation. They will also address issues like the nature of mission; its motives and aim; general revelation; the theology of religion; salvation and its socio-political implications; dialogue and proclamation; witness and proselytism; syncretism and accommodation.

Those who come from Asia, as well as those who feel called to minister in Asia, would do well to read books by theologians from Asia as well as the West, such as Dr Hwa Yung (1997), who is currently the Methodist Bishop in Malaysia, Dr Kosuke Koyama (1974), the Japanese theologian who worked as a missionary in Thailand, and Dr Vinoth Ramachandra (2003), who developed university student work in Sri Lanka and currently serves on the IFES Senior Leadership Team as Secretary for Dialogue & Social Engagement.

Missionary candidates must also learn lessons from the past. They are not the first Christians to go out into the world to share the good news of Jesus Christ. For two thousand years, others have gone out, showing great courage and determination. If the new generation of Asian missionaries will learn from them, their predecessors, they will be able to emulate their successes and avoid their mistakes.

Cross-cultural hermeneutics

As I travel I become more aware that Christians in other countries read the Bible differently from the way I do. They become excited about things I consider irrelevant. They understand things which are a complete mystery to me.

When I was preaching on the call of Abraham in Tanzania (Genesis 12:1-3), I said nothing about the curse God pronounced. I was strongly rebuked by a bishop: 'God promised to curse everyone who cursed Abraham. In Africa curses are very important.' He was right, but not only about Africa. In many cultures curses are treated very seriously and the Bible has many references to curses. An important facet of biblical teaching is that Christ has redeemed us from the curse of the law, having become a curse for us (Galatians 3:13). Jesus also delivers us from all those who would harm us with their curses, for he has triumphed over all the forces of evil (Colossians 2:15).

In many parts of the world, people follow a lifestyle that bears similarities to that of the Ancient Near East. The way of life of the Falashas in Ethiopia, among whom we worked for five years, was remarkably similar to the agrarian society of first century Palestine. The same is true in many parts of the Third World. People from such backgrounds find it much easier to understand and relate to biblical stories and customs, which the Westerner finds strange or incomprehensible. Sacrifice is widely practised in traditional societies. Ideas of kingship and covenant are common in Africa. Genealogies have a great significance in nomadic societies for your genealogy determines your identity and role in society. Dreams too are taken seriously in many cultures and are often assumed to be messages from the unseen world.

It is critical that students grapple with issues of contextualization and learn to discern how Christian truth can be expressed within a given context. How far can ideas, illustrations or religious practices be adapted from the recipient culture without running the risk of syncretism? The writings of S. B. Bevans (1998) and Paul Hiebert (1994) provide useful guidelines to different approaches that are followed in contextualization.

THE CONTEXTUALIZATION OF ASIAN MISSIONARY TRAINING PROGRAMMES

A number of excellent Asian models have been developed which provide a contextualised pattern of missionary training for others to follow. Notable among these are the Outreach Training Institute in India, the Asian Cross-cultural Training Institute in Singapore and the Global Ministries Training Centre in South Korea. The aim of these programmes is to provide holistic training that is culturally relevant and eminently practical. In my book

Preparing to Serve (1995) I set out to study these and similar training programmes, to examine the reasons for their success and to analyse some of their common characteristics.

Trainers

The key to the success of these programmes depends on having clear objectives and the right trainers. It is recognised that ideally those who train others should have served as cross-cultural missionaries, experienced the shock of living in a foreign culture and struggled with the problems of learning a new language. Those who direct such programmes seek to appoint those who are good spiritual examples in faith, in prayer, in commitment to Christ and concern for evangelism. They look for trainers who are willing to live simply and sacrificially, requiring no less of themselves than they do of their students.

Whether they expect it or not, trainers will be seen as models by those they train. Those who study under them will tend to repeat their views, reflect their lifestyles and may even copy their mannerisms! They will take their mentors as models. Consciously or unconsciously they will pattern their own spiritual lives, their family life and their ministry on their observations of their trainers. The effectiveness of the programmes depends on the character and experience of those who train.

Culture and values

Asian Bible colleges and training institutions will reflect Asian cultures and values. This will be seen in their understanding of leadership, in their attitudes towards teachers and in the educational methods they adopt. This does not mean that the leader will always be viewed as the patron, or that the word of the teacher will never be questioned, or that the contemporary patterns of adult education will never be utilised, but it does mean that the ethos of the training programme will differ from that of its Western counterparts and will not necessarily replicate Western leadership styles or educational patterns.

Ministry in Asian contexts, particularly in rural settings, will require different styles of communication. Formal sermons may not be appropriate. Villagers may prefer story-telling and practical application of the faith rather than cerebral academic teaching. Even in urban areas, preaching that is cyclical rather than linear in its structure may be more appreciated.

In contrast to the excessive Western emphasis on the importance of the individual, greater emphasis will be given to the family and to the community. Respect for elders will be upheld as a traditional value in Asian societies and fully consistent with biblical teaching. In patterns of relationship there will be an emphasis on avoiding unnecessary embarrassment. In the proclamation of the gospel emphasis will be given to that fact that Christ has taken our shame as well as our guilt.

Flexible programmes

The consensus of those who research the impact of missionary training and those who have been involved in training programmes is that all missionaries should undergo a minimum of one year's preparation in a specialised residential missionary programme.

Yet sometimes for valid reasons it may not be possible for a candidate to undertake such a programme. If that is the case, other means need to be found to provide the same breadth of personal, spiritual, cultural and theological preparation. Some colleges offer three month courses, evening classes or weekend sessions. Large churches offer their own training programmes though they are clearly not able to offer the same breadth and level of missionary expertise that can be found in a specialised institution. Some courses can be taken online. *The Perspectives on the World Christian Movement Course* (2009) provides an excellent foundation for some aspects of mission service.

A few agencies have developed reading programmes which deal with areas, such as the spiritual life or preparation for the family. They recommend that candidates have a personal tutor who can discuss their reading with them and provide pastoral care and supervision. In future greater flexibility may be needed in developing patterns of training and alternative programmes.

Whatever patterns of training are developed by Asian churches and mission agencies, everything possible must be done to ensure that candidates are fully prepared and equipped for the service to which they are called. Kane (1982) argues that it is consummate folly to send out people as missionaries who are not adequately trained. As the Christians of Asia play an increasing role in the evangelisation of the world, it is a matter of urgency that due attention is given to the preparation of those who are sent out on this great task.

NOT UNDER LORE:
REVIEWING ASSUMPTIONS THAT SHAPE CHRISTIAN
TRAINING RELATED TO WITNESS TO MUSLIMS
CAROL WALKER

Dr Carol Walker served with Interserve for 21 years in Pakistan and then Egypt, and later was on the management team of the Church Mission Society (CMS). She now lectures in Islamics and Biblical Studies on the undergraduate and postgraduate programmes at All Nations Christian College.

The gleanings that I draw on to review some issues and to make some suggestions in this chapter come from a mix of separate experiences, observations, associations and conversations. At various times over the last forty years I have attended training, led and shaped training, lived in South Asian majority Muslim contexts and stood back to re-examine my understanding of Islam. I have seen the simplicity of the Gospel bring life and liberty to the hearts of ordinary individuals born and living in Muslim mohallahs, and worshipped Christ in gatherings of believers from such backgrounds. I have agonised with loving Christian brothers and sisters about how to provide for longer-term needs of friends who have embraced the Gospel, and heard how practical initiatives taken in one place have not necessarily been possible or appropriate in another. My own knowledge has grown, though interestingly I am not sure that has impacted my personal 'effectiveness' in witness. (It may have affected whom I tend to interact with.) Over that same period there has been a vast change in Western consciousness of Islam and in the engagement of the church in Europe and America with the presence of Muslim peoples, but also in the numbers of followers of Christ in the Middle East and Asia who come from a Muslim background. Ease of communication, in terms of travel and the various forms of electronic media, as the globalisation process reached its astonishing momentum at the beginning of the twenty-first century, has been of major significance. The Spirit of God has been active within this, touching lives and communities, whilst fresh and heightened social tensions have also occurred. Given these things some of us may be more satisfied than others about the nature of training provided for Christians here in the

West, or within the Asian context, which is our particular focus. This chapter is intended to help us to decide.

REVIEWING ASSUMPTIONS ABOUT THE CONTEXT

Does Asia begin at the Bosphorus, or has it shifted East? When we consider the witness to the good news of Jesus Christ, Son of God, in Asia, what different social, political and cultural settings are we thinking about? Are the assumptions we need to work from in these situations, or with individuals, families and communities within them, the same or different from those that inform our relational interactions and witness to Muslims in Britain, other parts of Europe and other Western contexts in our globalised, 21ˢᵗ century world?

One of the reasons for entitling this paper 'Not Under Lore' is to highlight the observation that collective knowledge from a past era should only shape our responses to Islam, and the related training, to the extent that it is relevant for different and changing situations. Within Asia, Turkey and South Thailand are today, and always have been, very different places. The peoples of the Philippines and Pakistan may exhibit some habits and ways of relating that overlap, but the current nature of their different encounters with those from the lands of former Christendom affect their attitudes, aspirations, and openness, differently. Meanwhile, whilst places like Brunei remain phenomenally wealthy, others like Bangladesh continue to struggle with issues of extreme poverty. Wealth from the Middle East has funded the dissemination of more fundamentalist or salafi forms of Islamic teaching in Muslim communities across the globe. (Even back in the 90s I remember seeing new mosques in Western China that had been funded with money from the Arab World, and talking to young men in a madrassah in Urumchi who indicated that their teacher had come from the Middle East.) Access to literature and especially the web, as well as to TV and radio, has meant that the urban, educated youth, and others, are, today, seeking to come to their own considered understanding of life, faith and the ways that society is to be ordered. Tensions and demarcations between some Christian and Muslim communities have sharpened, whilst openness and sharing between individuals have deepened elsewhere.

A key question for us is whether these factors have implications for formal training in relation to Christian witness, and the nurturing of disciples of Christ? They suggest that practical witness should still come in many forms. Engagement in development, relief work and sustained medical care are important expressions of the love of Christ in many situations, and guileless testimony to personal experience of God's calling and provision remain vehicles through which the Holy Spirit makes Christ real to seeking individuals. Training should not over-complicate things. However, 'faith comes through hearing' (Romans 10:14), as the impact of TV, Radio, and the web demonstrates, and is facilitated by teaching and modelled discipleship. The things heard, taught and modelled tend to be what is learned. These can have been based on false assumptions.

REVIEWING ASSUMPTIONS ABOUT THE PRACTICE OF MUSLIMS
Amongst the 'lore' that may be shaping our teaching are corporate assumptions we, as Christians, tend to promote amongst ourselves. Some are derived from the kind of Islam in the local context where we have ministered, if not grown up in, or in which someone who has influenced us has lived and worked. I remember the first time I went into Hagia Sophia in Istanbul, and saw the large shields each with the name of one of the Rightly Guided Caliphs on them: having lived and worked in Pakistan I was shocked at what seemed like an elevation of men to a place of idolatrous reverence. I was also initially shocked on the Cairo Metro to see people reading their Qur'ans as they travelled, for I had had interesting conversations on Pakistani trains about the need to have clean (as in freshly washed) hands when I drew out a Bible to help clarify some point in discussion: that is, I had encountered Pakistani Muslims who were convinced that scripture cannot be read on public transport, and had at one stage taken this to be the definitive Muslim view. I remember, when reading Christina Mallouhi's generally very helpful *Mini-skirts, Mothers and Muslims*, (Mallouhi, 1994), at being struck by the way some categorical guidelines she gives are more appropriate for the Arab Middle East than the sub-continent. On the other hand, my practised skill at not looking men in the eye but talking to their shoulders, learnt in Pakistan, caused amusement and affront in Cairo! But then sophisticated Middle Eastern Muslim women have told me that no one wears a shuttle-cock burqah now: their world, and their experience of the teachings and practices of Islam, are enormously different to that of others living in Kandahar, but also Banda Aceh, for example.

Whatever we may read or experience of particular hard-line interpretations of Islam we do well to keep in mind that different Muslims have different views on what is true faith and what might be practical expressions of syncretism or ignorance. We do not share our faith with theories, but with real people - who may, themselves, need help getting beyond stereotypical notions about Christians! How many training programmes give consideration to Muslim perceptions of Christians, and Christianity, and the kinds of personal as well as practical steps that might be taken to dispel them? (I am about to give copies of *Jesus Through Asian Eyes* (South Asian Forum, 2011) to a group starting a course on Inter-faith work here in UK to encourage that kind of shift in thinking.)

Our corporate understanding of subjects such as women's dress, or their education, tends to be tied to what we also understand about shari'ah. Despite Archbishop Rowan Williams' attempts at introducing nuanced understanding of the term, I confess to having functioned on the understanding that the term reflects some kind of fixed body of, largely restrictive, even draconian, legislation. Though I knew that, since the eighth to ninth centuries, there have been four major schools of Islamic law, I had not absorbed the degree of flexibility which such a multiplicity represents. I had also taken expressed frustrations about the limitations of *ijtihad* (technically meaning making legal judgements, though by some used more loosely to mean interpretation) (e.g., Barazangi, 2004:7) as confirming that none but the *'ulamā* (recognised Muslim scholars of the law) are allowed to interpret the Qur'an in orthodox Sunni Islam – perhaps I misrepresent what I think is 'lore' amongst many Christians who have actually always had a richer understanding than I? Whatever the case, I have recently had my understanding of an event called the Mihna (218 AH / 833 CE), and the strictures and freedoms which that gave to Mu'tazilite and Ash'arite perspectives on the use of human reason in the making of legal decisions, corrected (see Nawas, 1996, Van Ess, 2006). What I find is that I bring expectations about legislation from the sense that I think I share in common with others who have grown up under the British Legal system: I struggle not to imagine shari'ah as a fixed body of written legislation, even though life experience already teaches me that it makes sense to recognise it as a shifting norm dependent on the power of a legal expert to carry community consensus. The weight of history may have fixed some rulings rather rigidly, even seeing them enshrined in national laws, but technically within Islam there remains scope for review and change. Thus, for example, when we feel concern for the plight of Christian and Jewish communities, because we know that they could face particular constraints as *dhimmi* where shari'ah is established, we are evidencing knowledge from experience rather than from a definitive knowledge of the binding rulings of Islam. How fixed a ruling is depends on the status of tradition to the interpreter, that is, the 'lore' they are following, whether they be a legislator or the community. Here is not the place to pursue details or consider what the implications of this are for British law: this is very helpfully considered by Julian Rivers in his contribution to the book *Between Naivety and Hostility: Uncovering the best Christian responses to Islam in Britain* (Rivers, 2011). The implications for training are that we should be cautious about giving categorical caricatures when we introduce sub-topics. We should not necessarily take what we have learnt from particular difficult circumstances to define all situations, and should encourage a constructive openness to discovering the ideas and practices of individual Muslims and their communities, without, in new contexts, prejudging outcomes.

REVIEWING ASSUMPTIONS ABOUT LEADING CONCERNS OF MUSLIMS

In relation to the Qur'an

That interpretation is not a closed practice amongst Muslims is evidenced by the increase in the number of Qur'anic Studies departments within universities in the Islamic world in the last 5 years. Depending on where we live and work we may be more conscious of increased fundamentalism, or we may be aware of renewed thoughtfulness.

A group of contributors from Iran, Turkey and USA, at the SOAS (London University) Biennial Conference on the Qur'an last November (2011), gave an overview of the recent profound change that is occurring, as the burgeoning Qur'anic Studies departments give attention to aspects of contemporary discussions about how to interpret text rather than simply inculcate students into the received knowledge of traditional *tafsīr*. Whilst some of these departments are merely taking a defensive stance to any attempts at scholarly critique by non-Muslims, particularly ideas about Syriac Christian sources or origins of Qu"anic material, others are engaging with fresh, sophisticated, interpretative questions. Scholars like Abdel Haleem, who is Professor of the SOAS department, and Mustansir Mir, who originates from the sub-continent, but is now Professor of Islamic Studies at Youngstown State University in Ohio, are giving an important lead to academically orientated Muslims in arguing the case for a coherent Qur'an (Mir, 1986) and setting out approaches to responsible interpretation (e.g. Abdel Haleem, 1993:71-98). There is particular emphasis on examining thematic coherency, building on the work of Fazlur Rahman (1980 & 1982). Muslim women scholars who have broken some ground in challenging patriarchal readings of the Qur'an have tended to build on these works (Hassan, 1985, Wadud, 1999, Barlas, 2002, and cautionary correctives by Ali, 2006). The work of the Buddhist Japanese scholar, Izutsu (Izutsu, 1964), who died last year, is also recognised as a serious contribution to discussion on a thematic approach to interpreting the Qur'an, whilst the work of the English convert to Islam, Prof Neal Robinson (Robinson, 2003), provides something of an example of how contemporary textual interpretation might proceed. Whilst knowledge of these works and their outcomes is probably still mainly confined to the academic world, and not yet exerting much influence in the Hindu Kush, the fact that the departments have changed so radically in the last decade suggests to me that training of Christians needs to keep abreast of developments.

Keeping abreast of the outcomes of serious research and study is a tricky problem. I have been aware that some amongst Evangelical Christians have heard about proposals by some Western academics that the Qur'an was produced well after the given-time for the life of Muhammad and that the material in it has a Syriac Christian provenance (Wansbrough, 1997, von Sivers, 2003:4 referring to Lüling 1993, Luxenberg, 2007). I have not, though, been especially aware of ripples of information going round informing people of counter proposals by other responsible Western scholars. There is a live conversation going on, with important reflection on what can be concluded with certainty about the milieu in which the Qur'an came into being. Helpful recent publications in the area include Keith Small's books (2011) on the textual histories of the New Testament and the Qur'an (one academic, the other at a popular level), Fred M. Donner's accessible distillation of the information we have about the origins of Islam (Donner, 2010), as well as important academic compilations (Reynolds, 2008, Neuwirth et al, 2010). The discussion, once again, reminds us that introductory teaching, whilst giving clear pegs on which to hang developing knowledge, needs to help students to appreciate where uncertainty resides, with best practice for those who will be involved in teaching and text-based ministries to include appreciation of commonalities between questions related to source and interpretation of the Qur'an and of the Bible. That poses a particular challenge in somewhere like Pakistan, where, still, few Christian leaders have grown up in an educational environment that fosters reflective practice and personal research, where access to resources and information remains limited, and where the wider-community understanding is that non-Muslims should not be making their own interpretations of the Qur'an. But examples of wise, good practice that I have seen convince me that it is possible as well as necessary.

In part my concern is regarding integrity as we live out the grace and truth made known in Jesus. Quite recently I was in a well-constructed introductory teaching session seeking to embody those principles, which yet presented the Qur'an as randomly gathered verses, and perpetuated the common assumption that the description of Mary as 'sister of Aaron' (Sura 19:28) indicates muddle over Mary, mother of Jesus, and Maryam, sibling of Moses and Aaron. I am persuaded that neither is the case. I find good grounds for thinking that most of the suras are actually single units of discourse (the problem for our understanding being due to our ingrained expectation of how ideas are structured). On closer consideration I also find evidence (Marx, 2010, and to some extent Mourad, 2008), indicating that the links made between Mary, Aaron, and more broadly with the family of Moses in the Qur'an, echo symbolism in Syriac hymns of the time convincing. This convinces me that the presentations of the mother of Jesus have a more knowing polemical purpose than those who ridicule them recognise (Neuwirth, 2010). I touch here on things many of our Muslim friends and neighbours may not have thought about (not least because when Muslims memorise the Qur'an they learn it in portions which do not match the divisions between suras, and may, indeed, think that Mary, mother of Jesus, was a sibling of Moses). This serves to warn us about our attitudes rather than, necessarily, to fuel our conversations, and to highlight the need for us to review our own 'traditions' about Islam and its scripture, which we pass on to one another, rather than cast aspersions on traditions being handed down between Muslims. They encourage us to be respectful of Muslims who are reviewing their own interpretation of their scripture and to want to see more Christians well versed in our scripture, understanding our own assumptions as we read and share its message.

Traditions and worldview

It, nevertheless, remains important to be aware that Muslim friends may be thinking about very different things. Amongst ordinary people there is every likelihood that their questions and concerns are related to traditions and local teaching. I was so glad, in Pakistan, to be in a role where I received queries written by ordinary young women. I remember being asked 'Is it true that when you have dogs in your house the angels go away?', whilst the most common questions from women and girls related to whether they could read scriptures during their menstrual period. Their questions give an indication of their worldview. They are an important reminder that whatever changes may be happening amongst the more educated, or are enforced by Islamists, those working amongst Muslims need to be aware of traditional ideas and of folk-practices too. Vivienne Stacey (1995) and Bill Musk (2003) have written helpfully on these things. We can benefit each other by sharing similar context specific material from East Asia. The best introductory training includes the use of case studies which, ideally, should be region specific, though many elements of folk religion are wide-spread.

As responses to Christian satellite TV and the like indicate, many Muslims are not really so concerned about gaining answers to theological questions but in discovering a God who is near, who forgives and who ministers to us in our need. I remember, years ago, FEBA Radio reporting that responses to two programmes they produced around the same time were the complete reverse of what they had expected. They had produced a teaching programme covering topics which Muslims raise in conversations with Christians (the term 'Son of God', the Trinity, whether the Bible has been changed), expecting this to be of interest to the Muslim audience: this programme brought a great response from Christians who found it helpful. Meanwhile, they had produced a programme about God meeting us in everyday life, being a present help in trouble: the mail bags for this programme were filled with letters from Muslims. Our encounters with Islam can cause us Christians to have to review our own understandings, which can be a great stimulus to maturing in Christ: this is one reason why our training programmes should not be rigidly didactic, but should be rooted in principles of reflective practice, equipping people to grow emotionally, spiritually and in intellectual understanding. Our encounters with Muslims should always take into account their shared human need to come to know the love of God. Let it be with robust argument where that is appropriate, but training should be geared to discovering how often it is not, and why the Bible encourages a 'soft answer' (Proverbs 15:1, cf., Colossians 4:6).

TRAINING PROGRAMMES: SOME COMMENTS ON CONTENT

Having spent a long portion of my adult life away from the UK I have returned to find that many respected training centres now major on courses validated by recognised degree awarding bodies. There are some benefits in the ways this provides for qualifications that can be built on and which indicate an individual's levels of competency to others. They can also be prescriptive and constraining. I feel a certain irritation with those courses which list the five pillars and the six articles of faith amongst their descriptors. Where a programme is geared to producing a summary assignment, all in a short length of time, these distillations can be so reductive, if not fundamentalist, in their absorptions. They have a tendency to turn life-shaping faith into a list of dogmas and legal codes without identifying keys to community and individual worldviews. Do not get me wrong. There is value in identifying core elements of belief and practice: it is astonishing what we do not know about one-another's faith. I remember a conversation, whilst watching the Wimbledon tennis tournament on TV with a group of friends, in which a mature Christian mission worker, back for a break from Nepal, aired her understanding that Muslims worshipped a multiplicity of gods! I also remember some Christians from Korea who had newly arrived in Cairo asking me if there were lots of Buddhists in the city, as they kept seeing people who were carrying sets of beads in their hands. (But then I do remember, on one bus journey in Pakistan, an educated, burqah-wearing, young woman, asking me if it were true that the Christians did not have any peace.)

Training does need to include review of core features of orthodox faith and belief, and with that to ensure trainees are in contact with Muslims in order to discover the place these things have in their lives: that is, how they relate to worldview. An excellent programme available for use in UK churches is Steve Bell's *Friendship First* (2003). Not only does its title promote the attitude which I here endorse, but it also signals the ideal way for the Christian to learn meaningfully about Islam. Serious Christians interested in Islam would greatly benefit one another if they were to share details of training materials available in their contexts that met similar criteria and which have provenly helped people to minister with confidence and sensitivity. (As a core text for a more extended introduction to Islam, Colin Chapman still serves us well in his revised *Cross and Crescent* (2007).

Where people know the location in which they are going to minister their training should give them opportunity to access information about local expressions of Islam, in order to learn of, and pray over, appropriate ways of engaging. God's church has been gifted with people who have different kinds of calling. Beyond ensuring foundational understanding, programmes should enable individuals to learn more in relation to their specific calling: development workers need opportunity to learn more of folk-Islam (still), whilst those preparing to be engage in verbal communication, including through the various contemporary written means, need to be on a pathway that enables a dialogical growth in understanding of Christianity and Islam. They need to be helped to tackle questions about their own Christian faith which emerge through encounter with Islam, even as they build up their knowledge of the religion practiced by Muslims. All need to know that they are on a pathway of discovery that does not provide some slick technique for winning the theological argument, but rather is likely to take them into challenges and spiritual battles for the sake of the Gospel.

In my own recent experience, whilst I have been combining particular family responsibilities with doing research related to Islam, I have been interested to note the number of other experienced workers who are engaging in advanced study. I think we have all become aware that there is more to learn. That will always be the case. But I also think it signals the need to approach mission as life-long learning, and to make provision for that in organisational processes and centres of training (whether geographically or virtually located).

Ultimately, though, the Gospel impulse is to share the love of Christ with those who do not know Him. Experience makes us aware that when individuals respond they often face serious challenges as well as the joy and liberation which Christ brings. Training for ministry amongst Muslims has to address issues of how to meet emotional, spiritual and learning needs of those who embrace Jesus Christ as Saviour and Lord. Anticipating the challenges requires the Christian worker to be developing a wholistic understanding of their own faith and of the worldview(s) of Muslims. Once more, there are both generic issues to be engaged with, and those which are context specific. Models from Bangladesh and Philippines have suggested possible ways forward for establishing communities of believers from Muslim backgrounds, but they do not fit all situations and individuals. Training for the Muslim world should not only be about witness, but about nurturing disciples equipped to be disciplers of others.

LESSONS FROM THE LIFE OF KARL REICHELT (1877-1952)

RORY MACKENZIE

Rev Dr Rory MacKenzie is Lecturer in Practical Theology and Buddhism and Placement Tutor at the International Christian College, Glasgow.

INTRODUCTION

Professor Brian Stanley begins his academic profile with the following comment 'My research and teaching interests derive from the conviction that Christianity is most true to itself when engaged in the risky business of mission' (www.ed.ac.uk/schools accessed 13.03.12).[26] Karl Reichelt spent his adult life engaged in the risky business of mission in China. His critics said that his highly contextualised approach compromised the Christian message. His admirers suggested that his capacity to make and sustain cross cultural friendships coupled with his ability to create a non-threatening environment in which to explore the Christian faith were significantly used by the Lord. Whatever else, Reichelt was a risk taker. Now, 60 years after his death, we examine Reichelt's life and work to see if we may learn anything about reaching out to the Buddhist world.

Karl Ludwig Reichelt was born in 1877 on a farm near Arendal, a city on the south coast of Norway. His father, a sea captain, died when Reichelt was very young. He was brought up by his mother who opened her home for house meetings and visiting preachers. Aged 18, Reichelt studied at a teachers' training college in Notodden where according to Thelle (1981:66)

[H]e encountered a more open, broadminded Christianity, which combined a sound faith with a deep appreciation of humanity, nature, national traditions, and the culture of the people. Such attitudes certainly helped him later when he had to meet other cultures and learn to appreciate the other national and religious traditions of another people.

Two years later he entered the Missionary Training College of the Norwegian Missionary Society in Stavanger. He was ordained in Oslo in

1903, went on to complete a semester of medical studies in hospitals in the capital and arrived in China in November 1903.[27] After completing language study Reichelt worked in Hunan until 1911 when he returned to Norway after his eight year term of service.

CALL TO SPECIALISE IN REACHING OUT TO THE RELIGIOUS PEOPLE OF CHINA

In 1905, Reichelt made his first significant contact with the Chinese Buddhist world. He visited Weishan monastery which was situated in the mountains and was home to 400 Buddhist monks. Reichelt wrote home, 'As never before I have been able to look into a unique world, a world full of deep religious mystique, but also full of deep spiritual poverty' (Sorik, 1997:73). Reichelt, along with his companions, spent one week in Weishan. They were treated with the friendliest hospitality he had ever experienced. This one week visit proved to be a life-changing event for the Norwegian missionary. Again he wrote:

> *Sitting with the monks, desperately eager to tell them of the Gospel, he found that his words were not heard. They listened politely, but there was no echo. It was as if they lived in a different world; he could not speak to the framework of their thought. He realised that he was simply unprepared and from that time on he began to study Buddhism seriously.*
>
> Sorik, 1997:73

Reichelt records another struggle he experienced on this visit. He was deeply burdened by the following question, 'Is it permissible for us to believe that God's Spirit can be at work within these bleak walls, where superstition and idolatry share space with the most exalted longings after truth, purity and freedom?'(Sorik, 1997:73). Towards the end of his week in the monastery, Reichelt believed that God spoke to him.

> *It was as if I heard the Lord's voice. It came to me in the form which St Paul expressed it in the Acts of the Apostles, 'God is not far from any one of us for in Him we live and move and have our being', and 'God has not left himself without witness'. Long before missionaries came to China, God was in China. The glimpses of truth and points of contact you find he has placed there.*
>
> Sorik, 1997:74

Reichelt concluded that what was necessary was serious study and went on to note 'I need not say that it was a changed missionary who walked down from the Weishan heights. It was a missionary whose heart was full of holy power and joy' (Sorik, 1997:74).

LEARNING IN LOCATION
Reichelt, having decided to devote his life to a special work among the Buddhists, began to study and observe Chinese Buddhism. He developed friendships with Buddhist monks and learned lay persons alike. In fact, Reichelt wrote that the greatest obstacle in the relationship between the monks and the Christians was that Buddhist monks had found the followers of Christ (both missionary and national) lacking in a sympathetic and gentle attitude to others.

He returned to Norway in 1911. During this time he gave lectures on Chinese Religion. These lectures were published in 1913 and later translated as *Religion in Chinese Garment*. On his return to China in 1913 Reichelt was appointed New Testament Lecturer to the Chinese Union Lutheran Theological Seminary in Shekow. He taught there from 1913 to 1920 and used his vacations to visit temples and monasteries, making valuable contacts and collecting texts which he studied in order to gain deeper insight into Buddhism.

REICHELT'S MINISTRY
In 1919, in a monastery in Nanjing (a city he did not normally visit) Reichelt met several young monks who were interested in what he had to say. Kuantu, a young monk, who had a 'deep religious spirit' responded to the idea of the Great Saviour from the West (Paradise). Kuantu got leave from the monastery and spent several months with Reichelt reading the Bible, talking and praying. He was baptised on Christmas day and was soon followed by a small group of others, including his teacher, and the abbot of the temple. Under Reichelt's leadership these new converts formed a 'Christian Brotherhood among China's Buddhists', based on the understanding that 'our Buddhist *Mahayana* scriptures point forward to Christianity as their true fulfilment.'

Reichelt returned to Norway for home assignment in 1920, full of optimism. He lectured on Chinese Buddhism in Scandinavian universities. His best known book, translated into English as *Truth and*

Tradition in Chinese Buddhism was based on his research and lecturing. In 1922 Reichelt returned to China after his second home assignment in Norway. With the support of his mission he started a Christian community which was organised along the lines of a Buddhist monastery. It functioned as a 'Brother Home' for religious seekers, especially Buddhist monks.

> *The monks usually stayed for a couple of days, but could extend their stay if they wanted to continue the study of Christianity. Every year an average of 1000 monks visited the Brother Home in Nanking. Here they could encounter Christianity in an atmosphere adapted to their own traditions, and talk about religious problems with Christians who were familiar with their religion and, moreover, regarded them as spiritual brothers, and 'Friends in the Way'.*
>
> *Thelle, 1981:67*

The following is a summary of some of the important aspects of the Brother Home (Ching Fong Shan). Wandering monks and pilgrims were received; if felt that they were found to be 'seeking' they were invited to stay for some weeks in the pilgrim halls. Indeed, if they were also young and well educated they would be invited to attend the school. During the first year of the school programme there was a strong focus on religion. This study brought the students to a decision either to become Christian and generally to stay on, or to leave the school. Reichelt comments 'We on our side plead with them not to make a decision before they are perfectly clear about the consequences' (Reichelt, 1937:164). Following this there was a theological course which ran for three years. Reichelt, (1937:164) went on to expand:

> *In this way the baptized, gifted and promising men will get a training which in due time qualifies them for teaching, preaching, and pastoral work. In this course the ordinary theological curriculum is followed, special stress being laid upon the history of religion, the comparative study of religion and the psychology of religion.*

In addition to this there were many conferences and retreats hosted at Tao Fong Shan where people from a variety of faiths were 'welcomed to sit down for earnest, religious talks and discussions' (Reichelt, 1937:164).

From 1922 to 1927 more than 5000 Buddhist and Taoist monks and lay devotees from all over China visited the 'Brother House' in Nanjing

(Reichelt 1937:162). In 1926, Reichelt parted company from the Norwegian Missionary Society as the mission had become uncomfortable with his highly contextualised approach and his view that Christ was the fulfilment of Mahayana Buddhism. Reichelt founded the Christian Mission to Buddhists, later referred to as the Areopagus Foundation. In 1927, revolutionaries, in an anti-foreign rage, destroyed Ching Fong Shan. Reichelt and his Norwegian assistant Thelle narrowly escaped with their lives.

Reichelt decided not to open a new centre in China. After looking around a number of countries he thought it best to locate in Hong Kong. In 1930, a wooded hilltop was purchased from the government and Reichelt named it Tao Fong Shan – 'The Hill of the Christ Wind'. A Danish architect drew up plans based on Chinese monasteries and a beautiful complex was constructed that demonstrated a creative attempt to indigenise Christian art and worship.

Tao Fong Shan was a place where Reichelt researched Chinese Buddhism and developed his missionary thinking. He travelled extensively, once as far west as the borders of Tibet but also to other Asian countries. The first focus of Reichelt's ministry, however, was sharing the Christian message with religious visitors. He and his assistants invited monks from China for visits. Some became Christian, a number becoming workers in his mission. Reichelt (1937:163) comments:

> One of the most interesting gatherings in our institute on Tao Fong Shan is the weekly evening meetings, when sometimes pilgrims and students from the different regions of East Asia tell how they were guided to come to this mountain. Their thrilling tales prove that our journeys, the distribution of literature, the wide correspondence maintained and, last but not least, the accounts given by the monks who have been here are all means in the hands of God for upbuilding the coming Kingdom.

The Japanese invasion of China in 1937 put an end to monks visiting Tao Fong Shan. After Pearl Harbour the Japanese captured Hong Kong and a period of hardship followed. Reichelt was allowed to continue at the monastery with his family and even carry on his ministry in the cathedral. At the end of the war Reichelt wanted to continue his work. He was, however, 69 and not in the best of health. He returned to Norway, leaving his assistants to continue the ministry of the monastery. Political instability in China meant that a return to the old style of ministry became impossible as travel was considerably restricted. In 1939, Reichelt was awarded the St Olav medal by the Norwegian King (Hakon VII) for his meritorious work. Some two years later he was honoured for his research on religious life in East Asia as an honorary doctor at Uppsala University (Strandenoes, 2009:129). In 1951, Reichelt returned to Tao Fong Shan on a short-term assignment. He did not return to Norway and in March 1952, Reichelt died of a brain tumour and was buried in the Resurrection Cemetery at Tao Fong Shan.

SOME ASPECTS OF REICHELT'S MINISTRY

Toward the end of his address to the 1938 Third International Missionary Council in Tambaram, near Madras, Reichelt took the opportunity to talk about the experience he gained over the previous 20 years of his contextualized ministry. During this time he had very close contact with thousands of ordained and lay Buddhists, Taoists and Confucians. Indeed, many of them had stayed at Reichelt's Christian monastery at Tao Fong Shan for months and, in some cases, years. He remarked that many of these men were contacted on his journeys (and those of his colleagues) to Buddhist centres and sacred mountains. Some of them, he said,

> *become baptised Christians, a considerably greater number have not joined the Christian Church but continue to feed upon the words of the New Testament and are bound to Christ our Lord in deep admiration, affection and love. These people have been acting as a vanguard for us in our work.*
>
> *Reichelt, 1938:99*

Reichelt went on to explain how Jesus Christ became the centre of the lives of these people. They were all searchers for the truth and the religious experiences in their former religion more or less prepared them for coming to faith. These converts to Christ heard Christ's voice because they were on the side of truth (John 18:37). According to Reichelt (1938:99) in 'many cases it was just the Gospel of St John which gave them the solution' as it pointed to the new birth which brought entry into the Kingdom of God. This new birth was thrilling to many of the pilgrims. After years of meditation in lonely cells and strenuous pilgrimages to the holy mountains and visiting great religious teachers they broke through and entered into the experience they dreamt and longed for (Reichelt: 1938:100).

Reichelt (1938:100) concluded by saying

> *What I have experienced through these many years in the sacred hours of conversation with these people has given me the profound conviction that Christ has been working everywhere through all the ages. We should, therefore, gratefully and joyfully use the material which He Himself has prepared for the coming of His Kingdom. That the result is genuinely right is also clear. For Christ Himself has given us the criterion 'Ye shall know them by their fruits' (Matt.7:16): a circle of people who through faith in the Lord have been set free from sin, fear and bondage and are now enthusiastically giving up their lives in service for Him.*

Reichelt's ministry was not restricted to 'words', it also included deeds of compassion. Strandenoes (2009:136) points out Reichelt's practice of giving food and money to those in need. He also tried to find employment for those who were out of work. His six months of medical and nursing studies in Oslo prior to his departure for China provided him with skills which he drew on in caring for the sick, for example those with serious wounds and opium addicts who had attempted suicide.

COST ASSOCIATED WITH REICHELT'S MINISTRY

In 1905, Reichelt married Anna Gerhardsen. The travelling involved in her husband's work and the political instability in East Asia meant she had to spend long periods in Norway away from her husband. 'It was not until after 1934 that she could be permanently with her husband and maintain a normal family life' (Thelle, 1981:66). Reichelt returned by himself for what was meant to be a brief period in Hong Kong and died there in 1952. Separation must have involved considerable hardship for both of them.

Reichelt was severely criticised by many of his missionary colleagues. He was perceived by conservatives as being liberal and syncristic. He drew fire not only from westerners but also from Chinese Christians who did not wish to be reminded of their religious heritage. A common complaint aimed at Reichelt's approach was 'You go to the "Brother House" to learn about Christianity but all you get is Buddhism!'

Reichelt's missiological approach, although currently admired by some practitioners, did not go down well at Tambaram. Henrick Kraemer's

(1888-1965) book published in time for the conference, *The Christian Message in a Non-Christian World* viewed other faith systems as an effort to evade, or placate God's wrath. This view was generally accepted at the time and Reichelt's sympathetic approach to East Asian religion was viewed unfavourably by many.

It was not only Christians who criticised Reichelt. His work drew fire from Buddhists who accused him of trying to damage the *sangha*. He accepted, however, that 'the most violent opposition, the most biting outbursts of controversy and condemnation must be experienced by those who present the Christian message in Buddhist ranks' (quoted in Eilert, 1974,144).

REICHELT'S MISSIOLOGY

The central plank of Reichelt's approach to faith sharing is what he referred to as the 'Johannine approach'. This had as its focus the Prologue with its proclamation of the *Logos*. His position was that The Second Person of the Trinity is not to be restricted to the historical Jesus. There was never a time when the Son was not. Reichelt followed the approach of Justin Martyr, Clement of Alexandria and Origen. The belief was that the Eternal *Logos*, the Spirit of Christ has revealed some truths to men and women from other faiths as they sought for truth. These divine truths, or *Logos Spermaticos*, are found in other religions and need to be identified and used to help people come to an understanding of Christ.

Reichelt argued that the activities of the Son cannot be limited to the time since his incarnation. From eternity he has functioned as the *Logos*. He was in the beginning, both abiding with the Father and, at the same time, linked up with humankind and the whole cosmos. He comments:

> *All that is true, good and noble in all nations and races, in all cultures and religions, has accordingly its origin in Him. What is the reason for this? The reason is that 'the light shineth in darkness' (verse 5). This is a permanent function on the part of the Logos through all ages, in all cultures and in all religions.*
>
> *Reichelt, 1938:93*

According to Reichelt, as soon as the pre-existent Christ was recognised, Buddhists would acclaim their natural state as children of

God. He 'had witnessed that such a discovery caused "an immense joy of recognition" among the converts' (Eilert, 1974 135). There is a strong sense of optimism in Reichelt's missiology. He was looking forward to a new era when the Kingdom of God would come in a much fuller way. Tao Fong Shan was for Reichelt a resting place where the Kingdom of God could break through in the minds of those who visited (Eilert, 1974:135). This optimism may well have been produced by post millenarian beliefs; yet there are traces of the bodhisattva concept of Mahayana Buddhism informing his practice.[28] Did he see himself and his colleagues as Christian bodhisattvas? He writes 'The aim of mission, of world-salvation is therefore: to help all that belongs to Him to find its way back to Him again' (Eilert, 1974:163). This is clearly in keeping with the bodhisattva's goal of striving for the liberation of all sentient beings. A bodhisattva is inspired and nurtured by the Buddhas: now is there an echo of being nurtured by the Trinity for working for the liberation of all in the following quote?

> *Fullness and vastness, and still no depressing feeling of loneliness. Because a Merciful Divine Father embraces it all in the warmth of his love, a Saviour and a Brother leads us along and an all-pervading Holy Spirit fills our heart with peace and makes it possible for us to give ourselves up for the most sacred and blessed task which human thought can perceive – the transformation of the whole universe into a Kingdom of God.*
>
> Quoted in Eilert, 1974:160

Reichelt drew heavily on Buddhist concepts and terms. He looked at his own faith through the lens of Mahayana Buddhism and used his knowledge in faith sharing. He also felt at liberty to construct a liturgy where the Buddhist visitor would feel comfortable.

SOME LIMITATIONS OF REICHELT'S MISSIOLOGY

Reichelt certainly studied hard to understand the world view of his audience and his approach was one of genuine friendship and inquiry. There were, however, some limitations. In my opinion he had an excessively high view of Pure Land Buddhism. Like Welsh Baptist missionary Timothy Richard (1845-1919), he understood Pure Land to be the purist form of Buddhism.[29] Mahayana was superior to Theravada and Pure Land was the highest expression of Mahayana Buddhism as it set out the concept of faith in someone other than one's self for salvation. Reichelt believed that Mahayana pointed beyond itself and ultimately found its fulfilment in Christ (quoted in Eilert 1974:164). This type of fulfilment approach and indeed, the using/reloading of Buddhist terms with Christian meaning require careful thought. Any building on and/or 'borrowing' may be viewed by Buddhists as Christianity colonizing Buddhism.

The concept of grace shines very clearly in Pure Land, particularly as every other expression of Buddhism focuses on liberation through self-effort. Indeed, when the Jesuits arrived in Japan around 1580 they were shocked by the similarity of Pure Land Buddhism to Protestantism. In dismay they exclaimed 'Martin Luther has been here before us!'[30] Yet Pure Land Buddhism draws on mantra and tantra and, in terms of practice, is similar to other Mahayana fraternities.

While Reichelt engaged with a number of key Buddhist concepts on their own terms and used them as a lens to examine his own Christian faith, the use of All Father or Christ for Amitabha, the Buddha of the Pure Land, is very much a penultimate arrangement and perhaps best to be avoided. There was a time when the Amitabha Buddha was Dharmakara, a bodhisattva seeking enlightenment. In contrast, there was never a time when Christ was not fully enlightened. Of course, one of the conditions of being a Buddha is to be born in the life in which enlightenment takes place in Jambudvipa (the general region of India) into a priestly or noble family. If we hold tightly to this, we cannot make Christ into a Buddha! If we do insist on comparing God to a Buddha we may use the Adi Buddha. This Buddha is referred to as self-originating and present before anything else existed. It may be understood as the original Buddha nature from which all Buddhas emerge. There is some resonance here with the eternal, unoriginated nature of God. Some comparison may also be made between Buddha-nature which Buddhists believe exists in all sentient beings and the image of god (*imago Dei*) which Christians believe is within each person. Just as Buddha-nature may point to the original source of the primordial Buddha, so the *imago Dei* points to God.

Lastly, we note that Reichelt did not respond well to criticism. In an interesting article about his father Notto Normann Thelle (1901-1990), Reichelt's right hand man, Notto R Thelle (2008: 84) writes that Reichelt did not welcome discussions about strategies and theological positions with his staff. He 'never checked the opinions of new staff, but he nevertheless expected them to share his views.' Indeed, Johannes Prip-Moller, the Danish architect who designed Tao Fong Shan felt that 'Reichelt's tendency to micromanage was an oppressive deprivation of freedom' and that his vision and empathy with others were 'limited exclusively to the sphere of religion'. Indeed, he said that Reichelt regarded disagreement as 'personal invalidation'. It is unlikely that Reichelt would get away with this kind of behaviour nowadays with new missionaries, and that is a good thing. If Prip-Moller's comments are true then it flags up the impact that criticism from colleagues, the Norwegian Missionary Society and the wider missionary community must have had on Reichelt.

FIVE LESSONS FROM REICHELT'S MINISTRY

First, Reichelt appears to have prioritised the keeping of Christ at the centre of his life and ministry. He ends an article written in 1937 entitled *Buddhism in China Today* with the following words:

> *We have one great aim, namely, to give the full Christian message, the full positive Gospel as it is revealed in the New Testament, using all the points of contact which psychologically may help the seekers after truth in East Asia to recognise Jesus Christ as the only way to the Father. We can afford to be broadminded because our work is through and through Christocentric.*

Second, Reichelt was genuinely interested in Buddhism but lived in missionary encounter with Buddhists. Reichelt's friendship with Buddhist communities was a new approach in the 1920's and 30's. He did not take a condemnatory approach toward Buddhists but engaged with them, and learned as much as he could about Buddhism. Despite his high view of aspects of Buddhist teaching and affection for Buddhists he was able to live in missionary encounter with Buddhists.

In a talk at Tambaram Reichelt indicates that despite his contextualized approach he had not parted company from the evangelical position:

> *I also hold the view that in our witness we must never lose sight of the great truths in regard to personal salvation so strongly set forth by St Paul, such as sin and grace, redemption through Christ, the living faith which sets us free and makes us*

partakers of the Heavenly Kingdom, with its wonderful vision of life in time and eternity.

Reichelt, 1938:91

More recently, Norwegian scholar Notto Thelle describes Reichelt as a 'pilgrim missionary':

> *As a missionary he was convinced that he had a special calling to preach, with a particular vision of a mission to Buddhists. Whatever he did – as a student of religion, a dialogue partner, and a preacher – he wanted to share his faith with others. He seemed to use every opportunity to deliver his message, expecting some of the monks to be prepared to grasp the gospel.*

Thelle, 2006:115

Third, Reichelt took a contextual approach despite possible dangers. Reichelt's monastery was a place where Buddhist monks were made welcome, he and his assistants wore a Buddhist type robe and the food was vegetarian. He developed forms of worship that would not be unfamiliar to the Buddhist monks. Incense was burnt, bells were rung and selected Buddhist scriptures were studied and related to the Bible, which was understood to be the supreme standard.

The Norwegian missionary wrote hymns and prayers that were couched in Buddhist terms. One example of Reichelt's boldness is found in a hymn to Christ included in the book of liturgy. Christ is there worshipped as 'The Great *Tao* without beginning and end (the eternal Word of God), and the original face of all sentient beings (a Zen idea but alluding, at least in Reichelt's mind, to the concept of the *imago Dei*). He (Christ) is the enlightened, the "Tathagata (Buddha) of the west who came to the world".' Again, Reichelt would often translate God for the Buddha and the 'All Father' for Amida. Japanese Buddhist scholar and Zen practitioner DT Suzuki (1870-1966) commenting on Reichelt's centre and the ethos of the worship there described it as a 'refined, religious atmosphere indigenous to the religious soul of China'.[31]

Buddhist practice usually begins with the reciting of the Triple Gem:

I take refuge in the Buddha
I take refuge in the Dhamma
I take refuge in the Sangha

Reichelt felt that a Christian equivalent to the Triple Gem would be helpful to visiting monks and proposed the following (a prototype of which he found in a Nestorian liturgy).

I take refuge in the Father of all goodness and mercy.
I take refuge in the mysterious, perfect Law (Tao/Logos)
I take refuge in the shining pure Holy Spirit

Sorik, 1997:76

Reichelt came under attack for this and other efforts at contextualisation. He was well aware of the dangers of an over contextualised approach yet was prepared to take risks with 'borrowings' from the other tradition. This is clear from his comment (1953: 59)

Syncretism and compromises in mission work are a real danger which missionaries must continuously guard against. On the other hand it is equally certain that there is a great danger lest they neglect to make use of the sacred material which Christ through His Spirit has made available in the life of the peoples and in their historical heritage.

He sometimes became more cautious as a result of the comments of his critics. That said, Reichelt was not overly concerned about the lines of demarcation between Christianity and other faiths. His first focus was making Christ known to Buddhists in terms they could best understand. If we were to use sociological 'set theory' we may say that Reichelt operated a 'centred set' rather than a 'bounded set' approach. That is, attendees belonged to the group before they accept the group's core values.[32] Those who stayed at the Brother House were encouraged to ask questions about core values and observe individuals and the way the Brother House functioned. In this sense they belonged to the community although they did not yet believe. Contemporary understandings of conversion/discipleship (e.g. in the emerging church) often say that discipleship precedes conversion and that for many the journey resembles the Emmaus Road rather than the Damascus Road. A centred set model was an essential feature of Reichelt's approach.

Fourth, Reichelt took the religious tradition of his audience very seriously. It was not simply a pragmatic exercise in order to know how best to contextualise the Christian message. Moreover, we can see how

Reichelt's interest opened up unusual opportunities for him and his colleagues. It may well be that the majority of missionaries do not wish to be specialists in the religions of their audience but Reichelt's experience suggests that they will be limited in their faith sharing and pastoral care without serious engagement with the religion of those they have been called to.

Fifth, Reichelt formed and maintained genuine friendships; indeed he had a genius for friendship with religious people from East Asia. He was often invited to speak at religious associations in temples and monasteries. In many cases some of the monks in a temple had already visited the 'Brother Home' or the rumours about the Christian 'Master' had reached the temple in advance. .

Indeed, Gluer (1968:56) goes as far as to say 'The secret of Reichelt's success in his encounter with Buddhists was not in his theological principles but in his warm personality.' Yet we cannot divorce Reichelt's theology from his personality. His openness to those of different faiths and his vision to offer generous hospitality on a 'no strings attached' basis facilitated the creative experiment that we refer to as the Brother Home.

CONCLUSION

Those who teach and/or mentor cross cultural missionaries may wish to reflect on how these lessons may best be modelled. Some missionaries from more conservative traditions may need 'permission' to study another religious tradition seriously. Those who come from a background influenced by postmodern values may need to be encouraged to live in missionary encounter with the other. Terry Muck suggests an approach of both cooperation and competition. We cooperate because we have issues of common concern and can help each other achieve a particular outcome. For example, clean water supplies, a better education system and improved health care. We compete because we have distinct belief systems and consider these to be crucial for the 'here and now' as well as 'after death'.

With Christ at the centre of life and ministry one can be comfortable with openness at the circumference. His guiding presence can indicate what is appropriate/inappropriate contextualisation. In Reichelt's life and ministry we are reminded that if we maintain our relationship with Christ his love will be in our hearts. If Christ's love is in our hearts then the people we are called to will be in our hearts. If they are in our hearts then we will be in their hearts.

THE 'MIDDLE WAY' MODEL?
TRAINING WITH CHINESE CHARACTERISTICS
TAN LOUN LING

Tan Loun Ling is Training Director of AsiaCMS, formerly lecturer and director of Asian Studies at Redcliffe College, UK. She spent five years as a pastor in Grace Singapore Chinese Church and served for 19 years with OMF as a mission leader and trainer. She is married to Kang San.

This chapter discusses the unique characteristics of Chinese culture, education, learning style, and values shaped mainly by Confucianism, with an emphasis on Chinese culture from Mainland China. However, it is important to note that the Chinese worldview is the seedbed of worldviews of many East Asians, particularly Chinese in Hong Kong, Taiwan, Singapore, and Malaysia. There is an attempt at the end of the chapter to apply the understanding derived from this discussion to mission training for Chinese trainees. It is hoped that especially non-Chinese trainers will find something useful to facilitate effectiveness in their training programmes for Chinese specifically, and East Asians in general.

CHINESE CHARACTERISTICS DEFINED
Dr Joseph Wu, Professor (Emeritus) of California State University at Sacramento, USA, describes basic Chinese culture as including the following characteristics: 'Naturalistic View of Life', 'Artistic Way of Life', 'Moderation and Harmony' (Wu 2004). To this list, which is not exhaustive, I would add 'Filial Piety, Loyalty, and Acceptance of Authority'.

Naturalistic view of life
Ancient Chinese philosophies such as Taoism and Confucianism support a naturalistic view of life. A person's duty is to live spontaneously and harmoniously in accordance with nature (Hesselgrave 1991).

Mencius, the first great successor to Confucius, told a story about a farmer who was worried that his rice plants were not growing. He went to the field to lift them up, thinking that he had helped them to grow. When his sons rushed out to have a look, they found all the plants had died (*Mencius* 2A:2).[33] The lesson: never tamper with nature.

Artistic way of life

Chinese culture is generally artistic in character. As illustrated by Dr Wu, in the Western world, medicine is a science by definition, but Chinese medicine is more an art. Classical prescriptions were known to be written in the form of verses.

Another illustration is provided by comparing Chinese and American cooking. Chinese cooking is very much an art, while American cooking is mostly a scientific procedure. It is claimed that one can never learn authentic Chinese cooking exclusively from a cook book recipe. It has to be learned through the imitation of a Master Chef.

If this distinction can be applied to the different learning methods of students, Western and Chinese, the fundamental learning method for a Western student is that of a student in science, following rules and procedures. But for a Chinese student, it is that of a student in art, the learning process is the imitation of models.

Moderation and harmony

What is the standard for proper conduct? The answer from Confucian ethics is moderation, avoiding extremes; the doctrine of the mean, or the 'middle way'. Moreover, those being influenced by the Taoist concept of the 'Yin and Yang' would see 'the two sides of any apparent contradiction existing in an active harmony' (Nisbett 2007, 175). So instead of determining who or which is right and who or which is wrong, they would find a compromise, a 'middle way' solution (Nisbett 2007, 184).

> *Together with moderation, the concept of harmony plays a significant guiding role in Chinese modes of thinking and Chinese ways of life.*

Chinese pay more attention to the social world around them (attitudes and behaviours of others). This is probably because a person's harmonious relationship with those in his/her social network (family, colleagues, neighbours, church) is highly valued. Relatively speaking, a Westerner would be more prepared to sacrifice harmony for fairness.

This concept of moderation and harmony may explain the inclination to create balance among conflicting components in Chinese culture. Wu gives an intriguing example of the Chinese attitude toward religion. 'One may worship the Buddha in the morning, then pray to Laotzu in the afternoon, and yet be "registered" as a Confucianist. Therefore a typical Chinese mind is often bothered by the exclusiveness and intolerance of the Christians toward their pagan beliefs' (Wu 2004).

Filial piety, loyalty, and acceptance of authority

For the Chinese, the key to living together in harmony is through filial piety, loyalty and acceptance of authority without questioning. As Confucius says, 'Let the prince be a prince, the minister a minister, the father a father, and the son a son' (The *Analects*, XII: 11).[34] Every person has a proper station in society and should conduct themselves and relate to others accordingly. This is the way to peaceful living in a well-ordered society.

So, knowing one's social position in relation to others (such as who is junior and who is senior in the group) is very important for acceptable social cues (such as who should speak first and who should have the last word in a class, or any meeting).

Filial piety and loyalty lead to one's respect for tradition – the established way of doing things. What was good for our ancestors is good for us. Elders know what is best. We are not expected to argue. Obviously, acceptance of authority without questioning could result in autocratic management, government, education systems, and social and family structures.

CHINESE PHILOSOPHY OF EDUCATION

The Chinese philosophy of education is very much shaped by Confucius' thoughts on education. These thoughts can be gleaned from the *Analects of Confucius*, a collection of moral and ethical principles enunciated by Confucius in conversations with his disciples.

According to Confucius, the most important issue is **the goal of education**, which is, ultimately to become a 'sage' (holy man), the ideal human model; realistically to become a '*jun zi*' (gentleman; a man of noble character). Thus **the core value of education** is the training of morality and personality; in other words, character building. Cultivation of the self through self-examination is the essential quality of someone who wishes to become a sage. In the *Analects*, Zhongzi said,

> *Every day I examine myself once and again: Have I tried my utmost in helping others? Have I been honest to my friends? Have I diligently reviewed the instructions from my Master?*[35]

Since growth is progressive, from one level of benevolence or kindness (*'ren'*) to the next, **education** should be **a lifelong learning experience**. From the *Analects*, II: 4, as interpreted (in brackets) by Yu Dan, a professor at China's Beijing Normal University (Tyldesley 2010), we have:

> *The Master said,*
> *'At fifteen, my heart was set upon learning' (diligence in study).*
> *'At thirty, I had planted my feet firm upon the ground' (taken my stand; able to confront society with confidence).*
> *'At forty, I no longer suffered from perplexities' (freedom from doubts and anxiety).*
> *'At fifty, I knew what were the biddings of Heaven' (knowing the will of Heaven; having an inner firmness of purpose).*
> *'At sixty, I heard them with docile ear' (having 'a sympathy for the world and all the people in it, that is, understanding and tolerance' (Tyldesley 2010, 181)).*
> *'At seventy, I could follow the dictates of my own heart; for what I desired no longer overstepped the boundaries of right' ('When all rules and high principles have become habit of life, you will be able to successfully follow your heart's desire...., a person must first be tempered by a thousand blows of the hammer before he or she can reach this state' (Tyldesley 2010, 183)).*

The *Analects* uses different categories for the various dimensions of growth: interpersonal growth, socio-political growth etc. So we see the **multi-dimensional** purposes in Confucian **education** and the practice of **life-wide learning**. For example, 'virtue', 'eloquence', 'government', 'culture and literature' are the four subjects in Confucianism. Confucius says, 'A gentleman should not be like a utensil. He should have broad knowledge and not be confined to one use.'[36]

In terms of **methodology of education**, teaching according to the competencies and interest of the students is one of the characteristics of Confucius education.

The Master said, 'Only one who bursts with eagerness do I instruct; only one who bubbles with excitement, do I enlighten. If I hold up one corner and a man cannot come back to me with the other three,[37] I do not continue the lesson' (The Analects, VII: 8).

A story is told of two of Confucius' disciples asking the same question:

Zi Lu asked, 'Should one respond immediately to a call?' Confucius said, 'How can you respond immediately to a call with your father and elder brothers alive?' Ran You asked the same question. 'Should one respond immediately to a call?' Confucius said, 'Yes, one should.'

Gongxi Hua was deeply perplexed, saying, 'I am puzzled. May I know why you gave two answers as to the same question?' Confucius said, 'Ran You usually hangs back, so I urge him on; Zi Lu advances bravely and sometimes audaciously, so I hold him back.'[38]

This also demonstrates that Confucius believes in giving personal attention to individual students as the most effective way to achieve his goal of education. We call it 'mentoring' or 'personal development sessions' in today's educational method.

Teachers should also teach not just in words, but also through action or conduct. In other words, they teach by modelling, setting an example for their students to emulate (remember the master chef mentioned earlier under the artistic way of life). His authority comes from his integrity and credibility. Confucius' disciples had great respect for Confucius precisely because of his noble lifestyle. 'The Master's manner was affable yet firm, commanding but not harsh, polite but easy' (The *Analects*, VII: 37).

Besides learning from the teacher, peer learning in humility is also encouraged.

The Master said, 'Even when walking in a party of no more than three I can always be certain of learning from those I am with. There will be good qualities that I can select for imitation and bad ones that will teach me what requires correction in myself (The Analects, VII: 21).

CHINESE LEARNING STYLE

Rote learning without thinking; spoon feeding from the teacher without permission to evaluate; passive and introverted learning: a preference for personal reading, sitting in lectures rather than interacting or debating with students and teachers, these are the common stereotypes of the Chinese learning style. Many think they are the outcome of Confucian education. But has Confucius been misunderstood?

Though Confucius gives clear instructions to his disciples, and guides them step by step, he does not compel them to go in any particular direction. He makes them learn through studying, reflecting and realising (being enlightened). The Master said, 'He who learns but does not think, is lost. He who thinks but does not learn is in great danger' (The *Analects*, II: 15).

One recent study of students from China in the University of Canberra, Australia, has challenged the stereotype of the 'Chinese learner'. Moore and Wang[39] explored the learning styles of Chinese with 58 modern Chinese educational leaders who enrolled in the Master of Educational Leadership programme. Approximately one third of the cohort were school principals, another third were administrators of local and provincial Education Departments, and the rest were university administrators and academics.

When asked for their views on selected readings from the literature that described the 'Chinese learner', drawing on their own learning experience, this was the result:

There was honest recognition that they did prefer some structured and teacher-led delivery. They also found that a teaching style where the key principles to be taught were articulated at the outset and supported by evidence afterwards was an approach that they were more familiar with. However, they rejected the 'Chinese learner' stereotype, explaining that while some of their practices may 'appear' intrapersonal and somewhat passive, they felt that the learning style was really more reflective, systematic and thorough.

It was observed that the educational leaders in this study were quite keen and motivated to embrace new approaches to learning and methods of teaching. Approximately 70% of the students surveyed preferred to take in information in ways other than the traditional lecture style, such as engaging in classroom discussion, debates, and allowing students to draw on their personal experience to arrive at possible solutions. In other words, they preferred 'student-centred' learning to 'teacher-centred' learning. Their findings suggest that

The learning styles of Chinese students are evolving with the increasing change in learning environments that they are being exposed to. Although some individuals in our program were somewhat conservative and reserved at the outset, once they got to know their classmates and teachers, and a spirit of trust was developed, they all contributed and questioned energetically.

Moore and Wang concluded that 'it is therefore essential that the teacher recognise that Chinese students are able to engage in the full spectrum of instructional approaches'. However, they also cautioned that care should be given when introducing techniques that are unfamiliar to students.

The findings from another recent exploratory study by Huang (2005)[40] of Chinese international students' perceptions of their problem-based learning (PBL) experience, with student-centred activities as adopted in most higher education institutions in the West, seem to support the general conclusion of Moore and Wang. Positively, students in Huang's study found the PBL more interactive than their old learning style, and allowed them to learn on their own. However, some negative perceptions were also expressed. 'Uncertainty about the accuracy of the acquired knowledge' was the descriptor most frequently mentioned. In particular, the students had a large psychological obstacle when it came to debating a subject with someone older and more experienced or with their lecturers.

Other similar studies also found that Chinese students were motivated to try a more active learning mode than other traditional teaching methods. They believed they could sharpen their skills in organising and integrating information through critical evaluation (Chung and Chow 1999, 2004).

CHINESE MISSION TRAINING MODEL

What then would be an effective mission training model for Chinese? As we have seen, there may have been some misconceptions of Confucius' philosophy of education - a Confucian confusion - and Chinese learning styles could be more subtle and complex than we think. Training directors of Chinese today should reflect on these words of Jonathan Chao '…the Chinese mind is complex, and that the Chinese people live in a complex cultural context in a process of rapid change' (Chao 1999, 19-20).

We have also encountered Chinese trainees today who are interested in and open to new approaches to teaching and learning if only they could be better equipped for the task. However, they would wish to see more sensitivity and support from their teachers-trainers when they struggle with unfamiliar learning styles.

In my research for this paper, I tried to find if there are existing mission training programmes for Chinese anywhere in Asia such as the equivalent of Britain's 'All Nations Christian College' or 'Redcliffe College'. There seems to be none! According to Titus and Helen Loong,[41] veteran Chinese mission trainers, 'mission studies' in Taiwan is just one or just a few courses in a given seminary. In Hong Kong, the situation is similar, with some short internship-type programmes which are usually field-based, according to Rudolf Mak, who works with the US Center for World Mission and the Perspectives Global Service Office. His current project is to translate and bring the *Perspectives*[42] curriculum to China, to encourage Chinese Christians to learn about the World Christian Movement. In Singapore, the Asian Cross-cultural Training Institute conducts a 3-month course, and not all the students are Chinese though they are mainly East Asians.

In China, there has been a growth in indigenous mission movements. A Declaration of the Fourth International Consultation of the Back to Jerusalem Movement, June 1-4, 2010, Jerusalem, states,

> *We firmly believe that God has blessed the Chinese people with increasing global status and influence "for such a time as this" (Esth. 4:14). Therefore, we believe that "spreading the gospel to the ends of the earth" is also the responsibility of the global Chinese church. Following Christ's example, with a humble and diligent attitude, we should wisely use the present opportunities to serve the peoples of all nations.*[43]

Rev. Morley Lee, the General Secretary of the Chinese Coordination Centre of World Evangelism (CCCOWE) wrote,

Many Western missiologists believe the 21st century will be the time we see most mission endeavour done by Chinese people. Moreover, they also predict that by 2025, China will be the country that sends the largest number of missionaries out. Just imagine only if one out of every thousand among the 50,000,000 Christians in China will respond to the Great Commission, there will be as many as 50,000 missionaries added to the army of the Heavenly Kingdom![44]

Through my contacts with Chinese leaders in China and overseas Chinese involved in China ministries, I found that generally there are two kinds of assistance the Church in China would like from the Church outside. One is for financial assistance. The other is for training, though the response here is mixed. While some feel that they do not need help in this area, others would welcome it, but would want it to be a more formal, better co-ordinated type of training, especially on leadership and cross cultural mission. Numerous groups from overseas have dropped in and out to conduct various courses. But they are poorly coordinated, resulting in lots of overlapping and students finding the content too elementary. Also, these visiting trainers concentrate in certain locations, mainly in the central and eastern parts of China. They appeal for more trainers to go to the northwest regions such as Xinjiang. The overall feedback is that many in China are prepared to go and serve but few are equipped and ready. A large number went anyway but returned prematurely, or even worse, left behind a negative impact. Thus projects such as Rudolf's Chinese translation of *Perspectives* materials will be invaluable. We hope eventually there will be a Chinese version (not just a translation) parallel to *the Perspectives* produced by Chinese mission scholars.

CONCLUSION

My own reflection on this topic brings me to the following brief recommendations for the future of mission training for Chinese, predominantly those from Mainland China.

Rediscover the essence of Confucius' philosophy of education

Confucius was outlawed as feudalistic by the Chinese Communist Party after 1949. But in the last two decades there has been an upsurge in popular interest, epitomised by the academic-turned-celebrity Yu Dan, whose book on the Analects quoted earlier has sold more than 10 million copies. Many

Chinese would agree with Professor Yu when he said, 'In China today we often say that for a nation to survive and prosper, Heaven must smile on it, the Earth must be favourable to it and its people must be at peace. It is to this harmonious balance that Confucius can lead us today' (Tyldesley 2010, 16). So a training programme that reflects the values of Confucius will be very well received by Chinese.

However, we should note that for the Christians, there could be theological barriers causing them to reject anything Confucian or Taoist as Confucian-Taoism is often considered by Chinese theologians as a human-centred culture not pleasing to God (Ling and Cheuk 1999). Yet others believe that Chinese Christians can honour their rich Confucian heritage without compromising their faith in Jesus Christ (Yeo 2008). It is not within the scope of this paper to deal with the theological issues involved in designing a Chinese mission training. However, for the sake of discussion, I have chosen to apply some of the Chinese ways of doing things and Confucian philosophy and values pertaining particularly to education to the training of Chinese Christians.

As Confucius stresses, the importance of both learning (diligent studies) and thinking (evaluation and application), **mission theories and practical training should go together.** While imparting knowledge, one should not lose sight of the goal of training which is **character development.** As learning should be life long, there should be **facilities available for on-going studies** for workers, maybe through distance learning. Where **content of the programme** is concerned, there should be **both breadth and depth.** For example, with reference to the four subjects in Confucianism mentioned earlier: 'virtue', 'eloquence', 'government', 'culture and literature', in today's curriculum the parallels would be 'morals and ethics', 'public communication' or other skill-type training, such as interpersonal skills, 'organisation, management and leadership', 'social studies' and ' literature research'. Mission training should study social, political, historical, not merely biblical and spiritual issues, and from a global perspective, not only Chinese or Asian perspectives. 'For Confucius, the *junzi* is not only good, he must also be a great and noble person, always mindful of the affairs of the world' (Tyldesley 2010, 85). A programme with such breadth and depth would call for **a team of competent trainers** from different backgrounds with various expertise.

The **relationship between teacher and student** is a vital factor when considering matching the teaching style to the learning style. If the teacher is looked upon as someone with knowledge and authority, **lecturing** would still be an effective teaching mode. But as the teacher is also respected for his wisdom and integrity, **mentoring, spending time walking, talking, eating, playing and praying, living together in a community** would be some of the natural approaches. In my recent communication[45] with Titus and Helen Loong, based on their extensive experience in mission training among East Asians, both in Asia and North America, they concluded that **the discipleship training model,** where the life (of the teacher) impacts the life (of the learner), is 'it' – the ideal model. By giving such personal attention, the trainer could meet the specific needs of the trainee, patiently allowing him or her to grow in his or her own space and time, i.e. naturally.

Finally, we note that the *Analects* is full of simple little stories, 'not long sections of high flown moralising' (Tyldesley 2010, 82). Should there be **more narratives (story-telling)** in a class of Chinese students?

Retain Chinese cultural characteristics with contemporary relevance as new helpful approaches are being introduced sensitively

Contemporary Neo-Confucian scholars have tried hard to see things from a global perspective, taking in valuable insights from Western culture (such as science and democracy) though their guiding spirit remains Confucian. They firmly believe that the Confucian tradition is the most open, inclusive, and creative among the various traditions of the world. They try to work out a synthesis of the East and West. They will abide by the scientific process at work and study while embracing Confucian values of authority, family and harmony at home and in society.

Some East Asian Chinese deal with this dual worldview embracement through compartmentalization. They use paradigms from the sciences in their academic, vocational, and public lives, but follow traditional Chinese values in their private lives and subconscious mind. Non-Chinese teachers will need to understand and accept such seeming dichotomy in their students' behaviour.

Introducing new approaches sensitively could apply, for example, to methods which require students to be more interactive and assertive. The setting for this to take place must be carefully prepared and there must also be a harmonious closure at the end. Otherwise, they will not be at ease for the rest of their training time.

Perhaps a 'middle way' model for Chinese training is the way forward – something old, something new; something East, something West; sometimes teacher-centred, sometimes student-centred. All done in moderation and in a spirit of harmony.

BEING IN MISSION IN THE INDIAN CONTEXT
CHRISTINA MANOHAR

Dr Christina Manohar is Lecturer in Systematic Theology at Union Biblical Seminary, Pune, India, and Associate Chaplain, University of Gloucestershire.

INTRODUCTION

'Who do people say that I am?' This was Jesus' query about his own person. The disciples respond by saying that for some he is John the Baptist, for some he is Elijah, for others Jeremiah or one of the prophets. Jesus continues to question the disciples; he asks, 'Who do you say that I am?' Peter replies that he is the Messiah, the Son of the living God (Mark 16: 13-16). This is a confession that comes out of the realisation that Jesus was not only a man but was more than a man. He is the Son of the living God. This is certainly one of the expressions of the significance and relevance of Jesus' person in a particular context.

The significance and relevance of Christ needs to be worked out afresh in each context. In order to do this, the worldviews, patterns of thinking, epistemology, psychology and the spiritual aspirations need to be taken into consideration. The Indian context is vast and complex. The twin issues that dominate this context are plurality and poverty. In this chapter, it is claimed that Indian patterns of thinking offer insights into ways of being in mission in India. This is done by considering examples from Indian cultural elements, Indian epistemology and spirituality and from the writings of Indian Christian theologians who have already made efforts to express the Christian faith in Indian thought forms.

UNDERSTANDING JESUS CHRIST IN INDIA

Some Greeks came to Philip and said to him, 'Sir, we wish to see Jesus' (John 12: 20, 21). To see Jesus is the wish of Indian Christians too. India is a country that celebrates diversity and multiplicity. It is a cradle of many religious traditions. Plurality is a reality in India. The Gospel is good news about Jesus Christ. This has universal significance since the good tidings are meant for all. If this message is universal, it has to be contextual too. The

Gospel is dynamic and cannot be reduced to some set categories. Kasper (1976, 9) writes, 'Jesus Christ is one of those figures with whom you are never finished once you have begun to explore his personality'. A revelation takes place in ever-new forms in each context according to need and aspiration. The Gospel is not identified with cultures but can be expressed using different cultural expressions as the Holy Spirit leads, since 'the Holy Spirit is the divine imagination in cultures' (Mundadan, 1998, 228).

Robinson (1958, 121) argues that the relation between Christ and the Spirit is so intimate that 'the activity of Spirit takes new forms'. The Spirit's role in Christology is both continuing Christ's mission and complementing his mission (Hendry, 1989, 426). The Spirit's 'function is therefore constantly to render Jesus Christ present in all his newness' (Kasper, 1976, 256).

Indians wish to see Jesus as an Oriental and they believe that Jesus can be understood from the 'inner springs of an Eastern mind and heart' (Thomas, 1969, 88). This can happen when Indian approaches to understanding Christ are developed. In other words, it takes place when there is creative encounter between Christian faith and Indian patterns of thought. To be more precise, it happens when one learns to weave the spirit of India with the Spirit of God who leads us into the Gospel message in a particular context.

When I say 'spirit of India', I mean the inner core or essence of Indian soul or psyche or mind-set. This can be revealed when one goes deeper into Indian ways of thinking. For example, a close look at sculpt images in ancient temples reveals a pattern of thought. An image of a fox reveals its cunningness rather than its anatomy. Similarly, one marvels at the mischievousness of the monkey that comes through such art rather than the clear anatomical structure of the monkey. This gives an insight into a thinking that focuses on the 'inner self' rather than the external body structure.

BEYOND THE EXTERNALS TO INNER SELF

Swami Abhishiktānanda (1910-1973) whose French name was Dom Henri Le Saux, was born in France in 1910 and entered a Benedictine monastery in 1929. He came to India in 1948 with a desire to experience Christian faith in the patterns of Hindu spirituality. He was caught up with the experience of interiority that is predominant in the Indian spirituality.

Abhishiktānanda began to realise that God abides in the highest heaven and in the cave of the human heart. While the West seeks to contemplate God who is in heaven, the East seeks to contemplate the Divine in the deep recesses of the human heart.

From the beginning of his life in India, Abhishiktānanda realised the difference between Greek metaphysics and the metaphysics of Eastern traditions. The Greeks unravelled the mystery of God at the level of the intellect but the path chosen by Indians is an inward journey into one's own consciousness.

In Abhishiktānanda's words, it is realising the 'unique presence of the Self within the self' (Abhishiktānanda, 1979, 21). He explains this as a lightning flash within. The light of the Spirit within one's self. Abhishiktānanda's theology is a Christian appropriation of this idea. He tries to show that the Indian approach to Christ is through the Holy Spirit that dwells deep within the human self.

This thought pattern is not alien to the Biblical thinking as the Bible affirms that the human body is the temple of the Holy Spirit (I Cor. 6:19) and the Spirit leads us into all Truth (John 14: 16, 17, 26). Like Abhishiktānanda many Indian Christian theologians have endeavoured to understand and express Christian faith in Indian forms of thinking. This theological exercise continues to date, suggesting that being in Christian mission in a particular context consists in paying careful attention and regard to epistemology and the religious aspirations of people in a particular context.

BEYOND BINARY CONCEPTIONS TO INCLUSIVE WHOLE

An observation of Indian classical dance offers a pattern of thinking that goes beyond all binary conception of 'either-or' and suggests a 'both-and' approach to reality. Indian classical dances are usually always spiritual in content. In Indian classical dance there is an oscillation between pose and movement. This rhythm is a special feature of Indian classical dance. Kothari (1990, 13), a dance historian, sees a close relationship between sculpture and dance. Dance appears to be mobile sculpture and sculpture appears to be frozen dance. It includes the exclusive parts and takes the viewer from exclusive parts to inclusive whole since in such dances the static dimension and movement are co-related to suggest that an 'either-or' pattern of thinking can be overcome.

The 'both-and' approach resolves many theological issues. For instance, how do we reconcile the human free will and God's sovereignty? Or how do we explain innocent suffering? If God is all powerful, God should be able to control earthquakes, floods, tsunamis, tornados, hurricane Katrina or any other evil by which people suffer not of their own fault. But these happen and people die or suffer in many ways. If God is not powerful then God is not God at all. There is another related question about how to reconcile human free will with divine sovereignty. These are deep questions for which the answer cannot be a clear and a straight forward yes or no, right or wrong. Either God rules the world or nature has its own course without recourse to God. Either God predestines everything or God allows humans to exercise their free will. This does not seem a satisfactory resolution. The 'either-or' framework does not seem to resolve the theological dilemmas. Eastern thinking offers a more profound way of understanding God, the relationship between God, humans and nature by thinking differently in the framework of 'both-and.' A theologian or a missiologist dwells in the border between the known and the unknown. It is a beautiful place to be because there is so much more to know, to perceive and to explore.

SET THEORIES AND STRATEGIES OR AN OPEN FIELD TO EXPLORE?
The resurrected Jesus appears to Mary and when she tries to hold him Jesus asks her not to hold him (John 20:16). Holding the risen Christ in one form, in one way, in one mode, in one pattern would make the Easter story incomplete. It has to go on forever, since there is so much to explore and comprehend in the profound mystery of Incarnation.

The religious art which is called *rangoli* or *kolam* that women in India make every morning in front of their homes using rice flour, kitchen spices, colours and flowers expresses that divine reality but does not confine to one pattern. The different patterns they make such as square, circle, triangle, rectangle and other patterns that do not fall into any category, express that the infinite reality cannot be captured in one shape, one form or in one way. The beautiful fresh patterns that are made in the morning disappear by evening. A new effort is made to do the patterns again the next morning. It is like a prayer that is said new every morning; a prayer that acknowledges the paradoxical nature of the Divine that appears and disappears, that is not fixed, static and immovable. This pattern of thought suggests that no one pattern or mission method or programme is an adequate, appropriate or suitable way to express the risen Christ who forever appears new. Hence inevitably it takes us beyond one structure or one pattern of engaging in mission or being a church in any context, not merely in the Indian context.

CHURCH OR CHRISTIAN COMMUNITIES THAT CROSS BOUNDARIES?

Christ exclaims, 'when I am lifted up I will draw all men unto myself' (John 12:32). The resurrected Christ is an inclusive space who goes beyond all binary conceptions, crosses boundaries and barriers and draws all to live in many ways. Perhaps in the Indian context, we need churches that are inclusive communities.

The Indian theologian, Keshub Chander Sen (1838-1884) appealed for a Church of the New Dispensation. By the Church of the New Dispensation, Sen meant a church in which the Spirit works out a creative synthesis of the basic Christian faith and Indian culture. His call is for the church to take deep roots in Indian expressions of spirituality. Indian forms of churches are emerging now in many parts of India and Christian faith is experienced and expressed in indigenous patterns. The questions for us to ponder are:

Can a church be a place where people can be comfortable with their multiple identities such as Hindu-Christian, Dalit-Christian, Tribal-Christian and so on?

When persecution takes place in India because of conversion from one religion to another can the church be an inclusive space and a secure place to be?

In parts of India, groups of high caste Hindu believers in Christ meet in different homes to worship Jesus. They call themselves 'Jesu Bhaktas' (devotees of Jesus). In this context, mission as invitation, forming home churches and other new forms of churches or Christian communities without perpetrating division and exclusiveness, are the need of the hour. Discovering some common ground between Christianity and the other faiths that people follow, without surrendering the universality and absoluteness of Christ is a significant aspect of being in Christian mission. This might build bridges between communities and pave a way to form new communities that might cross boundaries.

BUILDING BRIDGES

The patterns of thinking, life style and the writings of many Indian Christian theologians have transformed the narrow exclusiveness found in communities and churches and set people in a broad arena of faith. Paul David Devanandan (1901-1962) spent his life building bridges between East and West, between Hindus and Christians, between religion and secular life, between Church and society, between individual and group, between God and His people. In a similar way, the major contribution of D. T. Niles (1908-1970) was the blending, not contrasting, of Eastern and Western thought, of Christianity and Hinduism. 'He absorbed from his Asian and Christian environment the hymns of Charles Wesley, the mysticism and devotion of Hindu jnana marga (the way of knowledge) and bhakti marga (the way of devotion)' (Creighton, 1984, 175).

Pandipeddi Chenchiah (1886-1959) made efforts to bring Hindus and Christians together. He speaks about one such effort thus:

> *I have started small groups consisting of Christians and Hindus for prayers for the sick. … The names of those for whom prayers for health have to be offered are circulated among them by word of mouth and each day prayers are offered at a fixed hour, giving a sort of common bond to the members. It is a rule that a Hindu should pray preferably for a Christian and a Christian for a Hindu (Thangasamy, 1966, xv-xvi).*

Nevertheless, such an endeavour was not without risk. Both Hindus as well as Christians misunderstood Chenchiah. Chenchiah recalled this collision in a brief conversation with his friend T.R. Venkatarama Sastri and writes:

> *He greeted me with the words, "I say you are in the position of a drum. You are thumped on both sides. Hindus go at you for your Christianity and Christians, I dare say, for your sympathy with Hinduism". "Mr Sastri", I replied… "I don't mind how hard they thump if only they drum some music out of me" (Thangasamy, 1966, x).*

All these efforts point to something much deeper and more profound. Mission is not a programme but it happens as we live along with others and penetrate and interlock ourselves with others in society.

MISSION: PROGRAMME OR PERMEATION?

The incarnation principle (John 1:14) of mission is a way of living among people. The Word became flesh and dwelt among us. This also is a pattern that is found in Indian spirituality. A Guru or a sage wanders in the streets; people gather around him, he teaches, instructs and guides them. Gradually a group of followers gather around him and if there is a need a small ashram is built. The Indian way does not start with building, strategies or plans. It begins with a person living among them. Being among the people gives a missional person (by this I mean a person with a mission in his or her heart) a clear insight into a broad spectrum of various religio-cultural and socio-political issues and the interconnection between them in a particular context.

Bishop V. S. Azariah (1874-1945), who was the first Indian bishop of Dornakal diocese, lived with his wife among the people, mostly among Dalit communities who converted to Christianity. A Christian teacher with his wife living among them made a great impact. Carol Graham, writing on the legacy of Azariah states:

> *Azariah was convinced that there did exist a culture, spectacularly Indian but not necessarily Hindu, which must be brought into the life of the church. Illiterate people learn best through singing and the Karnatica school of music, very rhythmic and tuneful, produced a fine collection of Telugu Christian lyrics, common to all the different traditions. The love of drama also was natural and spontaneous. Above all, the love of festivals, particularly those connected with rural life, provided opportunities for big gatherings (Graham, 1985, 17).*

Living among people, appreciating the positive aspects of their culture, knowing their psychology and forms of thinking, and expressing various tenets of Christian faith in the mode and tools a particular culture offers; experiencing the problems they face, and working along with them to solve these problems is a way of being in mission, rather than planning a programme on their behalf from the outside. Pandita Ramabai (1858-1922), a Brahmin, married a low caste advocate and became a widow when she was twenty-three years old. She worked along with people when they faced famine in 1896 in Pune, Maharashtra, India. She worked among people in different ways. She rescued many outcaste children, Brahmin child widows, orphans and destitute women and provided them a place to live with dignity. The home she established which is called, '*mukti* mission' still stands in Pune as a living witness to her work. Her model was Jesus who offered people spiritual, emotional and social salvation. She gathered seventy destitute women and trained them to translate the Bible into the Marathi language in a non-racial and a non-hierarchical way. This offers us a model of raising local indigenous leaders and local people who can work together in partnership rather than imposing leadership from outside.

PARTNERSHIP IN MISSION
In parts of India where secret Christians who worship Jesus abound, women are the secret ministers who care, tend, comfort and also lead the worship, prayer, and house groups in profound devotion to Christ. In circumstances where fear dominates and being a follower of Christ might engender many unfortunate events, the presence of an ordained priest or pastors from mainline churches does not seem a suitable option. Lay men and women work together to keep the faith alive. In such contexts, ways of being a Christian as an individual and as a part of a secret believing community naturally develop.

There is a strong bond developing between different communities and people groups within India. People from high caste work alongside low caste people to break the dichotomy between purity and pollution; Hindus and non-Hindus undertake peace marches to enforce non-violence, peace, and harmony among people.

August 10th, 2011 was observed as 'black day' to protest against the exclusion of the Dalit Christians and Dalit Muslims from the Scheduled Caste list. Dalit Christians and Dalit Muslims condemned the Indian constitution (Scheduled Castes) order, 1950, which states: 'no person who professes a religion different from Hinduism shall be deemed to be a member of a Scheduled Caste'. This is anti-secular and anti-constitutional since it contradicts two important articles of the constitution such as article 15, which prohibits any form of discrimination on the basis of religion and article 25 which gives a fundamental right to profess, practise and propagate religion according to one's choice. Dalit Muslims and Dalit Christians oppose this legal means of dividing Dalit communities on the basis of religion.

In this context, it is crucial to say that Christian mission is working towards humanising de-humanised Dalits. This can be done only in partnership with like-minded people who emphasise political liberation and social emancipation for all oppressed communities. Human rights activists, social activists, non-government organisations, people from other faiths and churches work alongside, fighting against all kinds of discrimination and emphasise political and social emancipation for all oppressed communities. This is a pattern already developing in many parts of India. In this context, without any effort on the part of Christians, the distinctiveness of Christian vocation will emerge while working along with others. Waiting for that instant is a way of being in Christian mission in India.

PARTNERSHIP WITH NATURE

It is not merely partnership with people but also partnership with nature that is an essential part of being in Christian mission in India. Citing again from Indian art and paintings, it is significant to notice that Indian festival paintings offer an ecological metaphysics since human beings are always portrayed as part of nature. In Tribal worldviews land is an important part of history, culture, religion and spirituality. Sacredness is inconceivable without land.

The seventh WCC (World Council of Churches) assembly that met in Canberra, Australia in 1991 had this theme: 'Come Holy Spirit Renew the Whole Creation'. Partnership with nature has as a prerequisite a sound and right understanding of the Holy Spirit who renews the whole creation. There are many green movements working towards preserving nature without recognising or acknowledging that they are engaged in a significant way in the movement of the Holy Spirit. This beckons us to conceive Christian mission beyond the borders of the Church.

GOD'S DEEDS OUTSIDE THE CHURCH

In Proverbs, Lady Wisdom (Spirit, Word and Wisdom are used interchangeably in Hellenistic Judaism) appears in the public squares and she calls out in a loud voice reminding men and women to listen to her (Proverbs 1.33). She declares her role in the public sphere, in the cultures of people, and in the political realm, providing guidance for kings and rulers (Proverbs 8. 15, 16).

Lady Wisdom's appearance in the public realm, her seat at a location of prominence and influence within culture, in the street, in the squares, at the busiest corner, at the entrance of the city gates, at the crossroads, the highest places in the town, reminds us that 'Wisdom is something not only needed, but also found in the crossroads and high places of our culture' (Boad, 2004. 11).

Lady Wisdom was with God in creation, she delights in the human race, its pursuits, culture and endeavours. 'Wisdom warns us not to flee from the public to the private, but rather to accept the invitation to engage in public discourse and academic pursuit, not only bringing wisdom to bear upon such discourse and pursuit, but also embracing Wisdom wherever she may be found' (Boad, 2004, 11).

Discerning the acts of God in the world and participating in God's acts is a way of being in mission. Perhaps, the Spirit is at work in fair policies, just treatments to all people, where rich care for the poor, in councils where fair measures are adapted to meet the needs of all people, in government policies, in progressive legislation, where loans are cancelled, where there are structures and schemes that speak about right to food, right to education, right to employment, in movements that facilitate human life and sustain nature, in religious and cultural renaissance, socio-political changes, where local leadership emerges from the marginalised communities, where voices of women are heard, most importantly in the attitudinal changes that happen in individual minds and in communities and where communities are built out of chaos. Hence discerning the Spirit of God's movement in the world is a way of being in Christian mission not merely in India but also in every context. Discerning also involves attentive listening to God's voice that comes through the cries and joys of people.

MISSION AS LISTENING

Jesus was silent when the lady caught in adultery stood before him. Jesus was silent when people accused her. Jesus was silent when a punishment was suggested (John 8:1-11). Is this Divinity in Action? Is silence a way of listening? Is this a meaning of liberation? Perhaps, mission in the Indian context also involves remaining silent, listening to silences and learning to read silences meaningfully. Being is equally important as doing. Chenchiah calls this yoga of the Spirit or yoking with the Spirit which means listening in the Spirit or into the Spirit. The significance and distinctiveness of

Christian mission lie in listening to this internal voice of the Holy Spirit which results in transforming self and community.

CONCLUSION

India is not closed to Christ but forever open to find Christ in her own thought forms and to respond to Christ in her own ways.

While I do not deny we need a model or method for mission training for the Indian context, mission training is an attitude, a state of mind. It begins with oneself. Mission training or methods cannot be forced from outside but need to emerge from the context. There is no one strategy, programme or action to be carried out. It is a continuous and on-going process, and mission happens when the Spirit of God, the human spirit and contextual realities integrate, resulting in spontaneous and faithful expressions. Where love is felt, words are heard and the eternal is discerned, and there Christian mission and the Kingdom of God is realised. I conclude with a prayer of Rabindranath Tagore for the Indian nation:

Where the mind is without fear
And the head is held high
Where knowledge is free
Where the world has not broken up
Into fragments by narrow domestic walls
Where words come out from the depth of truth
Where tireless striving stretches its arms towards perfection
Where the clear stream of reason
Has not lost its way into the dreary desert sand of dead habits
Where the mind is led forward by thee
Into ever widening thought and action
Into that heaven of freedom, my Father, let my country awake.

NOTES

[1] This chapter is an edited version of a paper given at the Fourth Asian Mission Consultation, 2-3 April, Wycliffe Centre, High Wycombe. For papers from previous consultations see Tan Kang San, Jonathan Ingleby, Simon Cozens, eds. *Understanding Asian Mission Movements*, Gloucester, Wide Margin, 2011.

[2] *Presence and Prophecy*, Church House Publishing, 2002:210.

[3] We recognise Asia is diverse, and we use the term *Asia and Asians* loosely. Hopefully, different Pan-Asian chapters offered in this book, engaging with a variety of Asian religious contexts, will offer some inter-regional and multi-faceted perspectives. Readers could further focus on respective areas of concern, for example, for the Indian context, Ebenezer D. Dasan and Frampton Fox, *Missiological Education: Theological Integration and Contextual Implications, Papers from the 13th CMS Consultation*, Delhi: CMS/ISPCK, 2009, or a specific mission agency review, Roger Bowen, Church Mission Society: *Mission Education Review*, April 2002.

[4] A revision from Johannes Verkuyl's classical definition of missiology (see Verykul, *Contemporary Missiology: An Introduction*, 1978:5-6). Methodologically, when engaging with the religious context, I am sympathetic toward Lalsangkima Pachuau's exposition of theology of religion as an integrating principle for missiology, see 'Missiology in a Pluralistic World: The place of Mission Study in Theological Education,' *International Review of Mission*, 89/No. 355 (October 2000): 539-555. For an anthropological approach, see the recent web discussion by Robert Priest who defines missiology, as 'an interdisciplinary discipline which, through research, writing and teaching, furthers the acquisition, development, and transmission of theologically-informed, contextually grounded, and ministry-oriented knowledge and understanding, with the goal of helping and correcting Christians, and Christian institutions, involved in the doing of Christian mission,' in 'What in the world is missiology?' Available from: http://www.missiologymatters.com/2012/ 03/07/what-in-the-world-is-missiology/ [accessed on 20th March, 2012]. With regard to the future of missiology, I foresee the increased importance and value of socio-political discourses and globalisation studies in analysing and understanding mission in the global and post-colonial context. In the final analysis, we seek 'God's wisdom in complex mission situations' that is biblically grounded, theologically informed,

and contextually sensitive. These presuppositions undergird the concept of 'contextual mission training.'

[5] The section on fragmentation of theological education is a revision from an earlier paper, see Tan Kang San, 'In Search of Contextualised Training Models for the Chinese Christian Diaspora in Britain,' Plenary paper presented at Lausanne Educator Conference in Europe, at Oxford Centre for Mission Studies, 16th April, 2010, published in *Transformation: An International Journal of Holistic Mission Studies*, 28(1): 29-41.

[6] Robert Banks, *Reenvisioning Theological Education: Exploring a Missional Alternative to Theological Education*, Grand Rapids: Eerdmans, 1999, criticises Farley's proposal of *theologia* for lacking missional orientation and still being limited in its bias toward the intellectual dimension of education.

[7] Tan Kang San, 'Why Evangelicals are unsuccessful among world religions?' Unpublished paper presented at Global Network for Centres of World Mission, Seoul, South Korea, 29th November to 3rd December, 2011; accepted for publication by *International Journal for Frontier Mission*, 2012.

[8] Italics mine.

[9] Global diversity in the community of learning is a critical component for intercultural learning, which is difficult to achieve in regional centres. We seldom have Africans studying in Asia, and Asians studying in Latin America. Britain's attractiveness as a centre for mission training due to this key criterion of student diversity has now been rendered increasingly difficult due to visa restrictions.

[10] See David Harley's good survey on 'Missionary Training in the United Kingdom (1910-1981)' in *Missionary Training: The History of All Nations Christian College*, Boekencentrum, 25-72.

[11] For example, Joint Information Service of ETE/WCC and WOCATI, Report on 'Theological Education in World Christianity,' 2009.

[12] For example, revision of 'Critical Asian Principle' by ATESEA as a guide for a more contextual curriculum, http://www.atesea.net/guidelines/guidelines-for-doing-theologies-in-asia/ [accessed 1st March, 2012].

[13] Sidney Rooy, 'Historical Models of Theological Education,'" in Rene Padilla, *New Alternatives in Theological Education*, Oxford: Latin American Fraternity, 1988:51-72.

[14] 'Challenges and Opportunities in Theological Education in the 21st Century: Pointers for a new international debate on Theological Education,' The Joint Information Service of ETE and WOCATI, 2009:17.

[15] See various works by Paul Hiebert, notably, *Transforming Worldviews: How people change*, Grand Rapids: Baker Academic, 2008.

[16] For example, works by mission theologians (David Bosch, Stephen Bevans, Robert Schreiter, Charles Van Engen, Kwame Bediako), mission historians (Andrew Walls, Lamin Sanneh, Samuel Moffatt, Michael Poon), anthropologists (Charles Kraft, Paul Hiebert, Robert Priest), Asian contextual theologians (Sebastian Kim, Kosuke Koyama, CS Song, Hwa Yung), post-colonial theologians (R.S. Sugirtharajah, Vinoth Ramachandra, Jonathan Ingleby), theologians of religions (Gavin D'Costa, Velli-Matti Karkanen), Christian scholars on Islam (Kenneth Cragg, Colin Chapman) and mission strategists.

[17] Although still limited for the non-English speaking world.

[18] The Board of Mission of the Archbishop's Council, *Presence and Prophecy*, Church House Publishing and Churches Together in Britain and Ireland 2002:210.

[19] I am not intending to enter the discussion as to when the name Yahweh entered the religious vocabulary of the patriarchs. The Biblical record seems to contradict itself! Compare the references just cited with Exodus 6:3. I am not concerned here, however, with the history so much as the fact that the writer of Genesis could put the two names together in the way that he does.

[20] For this whole discussion see Brett (2009) 45-61.

[21] I have written about this novel before. See Ingleby, J. 'Small communities and the impact of modernity: a meditation on Mario Vargas Llosa's *El Hablador* and its meaning for mission today' in *Transformation* Vol 24 No 1, January 2007.

[22] For the whole of this discussion on 'construction' see Brueggemann (1993) 1-17.

[23] To explore further the approach to mission adopted by the Jesuits in Japan and then in China see Andrew Ross's superb *A Vision Betrayed*, a wonderful example of missiological history.

[24] And for more examples of this, see *Christian Theology in Asia*, edited by Sebastian Kim and *Christianities in Asia*, edited by Peter Phan.

[25] For more on this see the very detailed treatment in John Howes *Japan's Modern Prophet*.

[26] Director of the Centre for the Study of Word Christianity, New College, University of Edinburgh.

[27] According to Standenoes (2009: 127) eight of the 1902 ordinands from the School of Missionary and Theology were ordained together in Oslo. On that occasion Reichelt preached from Acts 10:42-3.

[28] Post millenarianists generally look forward to a 'golden age' of Gospel advance and peace on earth prior to the Lord's return.

[29] Pure Land Buddhists believe that trusting in the Amitabha (Amida) Buddha means one will be reborn in his pure land, Sukhavati, in the western region of the universe. This rebirth is not due to personal *karma* but rather a transfer of Amitabha's merit stimulated by prayer/trust. Enlightenment may be gained in this final life in Sukhavati due to the conducive conditions which exist there.

[30] For an interesting account of the Jesuit mission in China and Japan see Andrew Ross, 1994 *Vision Betrayed: The Jesuits in Japan and China 1542-1742*, Edinburgh: Edinburgh University Press.

[31] Reichelt had a high view of Suzuki as a scholar and a Buddhist practitioner. Eilert (1974:126) comments that in 1927 Reichelt 'was happy to meet Suzuki whose books I have read so often'. Indeed, Eilert goes on to suggest that there is an element of Zen to be seen in Reichelt's writing which suggests that he was influenced by Suzuki.

[32] For a good introduction on 'sets' see pp.180-2 of Stuart Murray, *Church Planting*, Milton Keynes: Paternoster Press, 1998. We briefly mentioned the 'centred set' approach and used it to describe the Brother House method of operating. Some churches operate on a 'bounded set' model. This approach keeps clear boundaries and maintains the integrity of the community by excluding any whose beliefs or behaviour are unacceptable. New members are inducted into the doctrinal beliefs and practices of the church. An advantage of this approach is that it provides structure and order and issues are black and white. A disadvantage may be that the setting of excessively rigid boundaries may marginalise people who have questions about belief and/or practice. If we emphasize a culture of conformity (for whatever reason) then we may marginalize people unnecessarily, or people may marginalize themselves e.g. saying I can't belong to this group. Another approach would be the 'fuzzy-set'. Not only is this model without significant boundaries, it has no clear values at its centre. A wide range of behaviour is tolerated in this approach and there are dangers of compromise and confusion associated with this.

[33] The *Mencius* is a record of conversations between Mencius and rulers of the feudal states, disciples, and philosophical adversaries; a selection could be found in Theodore de Bary, Wm. and Irene Bloom, compiled, *Sources of Chinese Tradition: from earliest times to 1600, Volume One, 2nd edition*. New York: Columbia University Press, 1999, 116-158.

[34] Unless specifically mentioned otherwise, all quotations from the *Confucius*

Analects are from the translation by Arthur Waley, in Pelikan (ed), *Sacred Writings, Confucianism: The Analects of Confucius*, New York: Book-of-The-Month Club, 1992.
[35] *Analects of Confucius*, Beijing Foreign Language Printing House, 1994, 3 http://www.china-review.com/sao.asp?id=2082 (accessed 19.3.2012).
[36] *Analects of Confucius*, Beijing Foreign Language Printing House, 1994, 19, http://www.china-review.com/sao.asp?id=2082 (accessed 19.3.2012).
[37] Metaphor from laying out of field-plots? (Pelikan 1992).
[38] *Analects of Confucius*, Beijing Foreign Language Printing House, 1994, 196-197, http://www.china-review.com/sao.asp?id=2082 (accessed 19.3.2012).
[39] Moore and Wang. *Adult Learning Styles of Modern Chinese Educational Learners: Challenging the Stereotype*, University of Canberra, ACT 2601, Australia, http://www.aare.edu.au/07pap/moo07557.pdf (accessed 19.3.2012).
[40] Huang, R. (2005) 'Chinese International Students' Perceptions of the Problem-Based Learning Experience,' *Journal of Hospitality, Leisure, Sport and Tourism Education* 4(2), 36-43, www.hlst.heacademy.ac.uk/johlste (accessed 20.3.2012).
[41] Dr Titus Loong, former Dean of Asian Cross-cultural Training Institute in Singapore, Director of Wecare Centre , Hong Kong; Helen Loong, Co-founder of Wecare Centre; both are World Venture missionaries to Asia.
[42] Winter, Ralph and Steven Hawthorne, ed., *Perspectives on the World Christian Movement: A Reader*, 3rd Edition, Pasadena: William Carey Library, 1999
[43] http://www.gcciusa.org/Chinese/b5_publications/GCB/2010/Aug/P22.pdf (accessed 20.3.12).
[44] To read his full article and more about CCCOWE, go to http://www.cccowe.org/eng/
[45] Email communication on 12.11.2011.

SELECTED BIBLIOGRAPHY

Abdel Haleem, M.A.S., 1993, 'Context and internal relationships: keys to quranic exegesis' in Hawting and Shareef (eds.), *Approaches to the Qur'an*, London: Routledge

Abhishiktānanda, 1979, *The Secrets of Arunachala*, Delhi: ISPCK

Ali, Kecia, 2006, *Sexual Ethics & Islam*, Oxford: One World, 2006

Barlas, Asma, 2002, *'Believing Women' in Islam*, Austin: University of Texas Press

Barazangi, Nimat Hafez, 2004, *Woman's Identity and the Qur'an*, Gainesville: U. of Florida

Bauman, Z.,1992, *Intimations of Postmodernity*, London: Routledge

Bell, Steve, 2003, *Friendship First*, Milton Keynes: Interserve

Bevans, S. 2010, *Models of Contextual Theology*, Maryknoll: Orbis

Boad, J. M., 2004, 'The Delight of Wisdom' *Themelios*, 30(1), 4-11

Bosch, D., 1982, 'Theological education in missionary perspective' in *Missiology* X/1 (January), 17-19

_____ 1991, *Transforming Mission*, Maryknoll: Orbis

Brett, M.G., 2009, *Decolonizing God*, Sheffield: Sheffield Phoenix Press

Brueggemann W, 1993, *The Bible and the Postmodern Imagination*, London: SCM

Chao, Jonathan, 1999, 'The Gospel and Culture in Chinese History' in Ling and Bieler (eds), *Chinese Intellectuals and the Gospel*, Canada: China Horizon and Horizon Ministries

Chapman, Colin, 2007, *Cross and Crescent*, Leicester: IVP

Cheesman, n.d., 'Is Professional a suitable adjective for Theological Education' available from: <http://www.theologicaleducation.org/docs/ resource1.pdf > [5th July, 2009], 1-7

Chung, J. C. C. and Chow, S. M. K., 1999, 'Imbedded PBL in an Asian Context: Opportunities and Challenges', *Proceedings of the 1st Asia-Pacific Conference on Problem-Based Learning*, December 9-11, 1999, Hong Kong, 35-46

_____ 2004, 'Promoting student learning through a student-centred problem-based learning subject curriculum' in *Innovations in Education and Teaching* 41(2), 157-168

Cook M et al. 2010, *Local Theology for the Global Church*, Pasadena: William Carey Library

Creighton, L., 1984, 'The Legacy of D. T. Niles', *IBMR*, 8(4), 174-178

Donner, Fred M., 2010, *Muhammad and the Believers*, Cambridge, Mass.: Harvard U. P.

Eilert, Hakan, 1974, *Boundlessness: Studies in Karl Ludvig Reichelt's Missionary*

Thinking with Special Regard to the Buddhist Christian Encounter, Arhus: Forlaget Arcs

Endō S, 1982, *Silence* (first KI edition) Tokyo: Kodansha International

Farley, E., 1994, *Theologia: The Fragmentation and Unity of Theological Education,* Minneapolis: Augsburg Fortress

Flemming, D., 2005, *Contextualization in the New Testament,* Leicester: Apollos

Gergen, K.J., 1999, *An Invitation to Social Construction* London: Sage

Gluer W, 1968, 'The Encounter between Christianity and Chinese Buddhism during the 19th Century and the First Half of the 20th Century' in *Ching Feng* Vol. XI No 3, 39-57

Graham, C., 1985, 'The Legacy of V. S. Azariah' *IBMR,* 9(1), 15-19

Harley, D., 1995, *Preparing to Serve,* Pasadena: William Carey Library

Hassan, Riffat, 1985, 'Made from Adam's Rib: The Woman's Creation Question', *Al-Mushir, Theological Journal of the Christian Study Centre, Rawalpindi, Pakistan* (Autumn), 124-56

Hay, R. et al., 2007, *Worth Keeping,* Pasadena: William Carey

Hendry, S. G., 1957, *The Holy Spirit in Christian Theology,* London: SCM

Hesselgrave, David, 1991, *Communicating Christ Cross Culturally,* Grand Rapids: Zondervan

Hewitt, M., 2004, 'Critical Theory' in *Blackwell Companion to Political Theology,* Oxford: Blackwell

Hiebert, P., 1994, *Anthropological Reflections on Missiological Issues,* Grand Rapids: Baker.

_____ 2008, *Transforming Worldviews,* Grand Rapids: Baker Academic

Hood R.E., 1990, *Must God Remain Greek?,* Minneapolis: Fortress Press

Howes JF, 2005, *Japan's Modern Prophet – Uchimura Kanzō,* Vancouver: UBC Press

Hwa Yung, 1997, *Mangoes or Bananas?,* Carlisle: Regnum

_____ 2008, 'The Gospel is the power of God for everyone who believes' in Marks, D. (ed.), *Shaping a Global Theological Mind,* Aldershot: Ashgate

Ingleby J., 2010, *Naming the Frame,* Gloucester: Wide Margin

Izutsu, Toshihiko, 1964, *God and Man in the Koran,* Tokyo: The Keio Institute

Kane, J. H., 1982, *A Concise History of the Christian World Mission,* Grand Rapids: Baker

Kasper, W., 1976, *Jesus the Christ,* London: Burns & Oats

Kelsey, D., 1992, *What is so theological about theological education?,* Westminster: John Knox

Kim S (ed.), 2008, *Christian Theology in Asia,* Cambridge: CUP

Kothari, S., 1990, *Odissi: Indian Classical Dance Art,* Bombay: Marg Publications

Koyama, K., 1974, *Waterbuffalo Theology,* London: SCM

Laing, M., 2009, 'Recovering Missional Ecclesiology in Theological Education' in *Missiological Education: Theological Integration and Contextual Implications,* Delhi: CMS/ISPCK

Ling, S. & Cheuk, C, 1999, *The 'Chinese' Way of Doing Things,* San Gabriel, CA and Vancouver, BC: China Horizon and Horizon Ministries Canada

Lüling, G., 1993, *Über den Urkoran. Ansatze zu Rekonstruktion der vorislamisch-christlichen Strophenlieder im Koran,* 2nd edn., Erlangen: Verlagsbuchhandlung H. Lüling

Luxenberg, C., 2007, *The Syro-Aramaic Reading of the Koran,* Berlin: Verlag Hans Schiller

McGrath, 1993, *The Renewal of Anglicanism,* London: SPCK
_____ 1997, *Christian Theology - An Introduction* (2nd Ed.), Oxford: Blackwell

Mallouhi, Christina, 1994, *Mini-skirts, Mothers and Muslim,* n.p.

Marx, Michael, 2010, 'Glimpses of a Mariology in the Qur'an' in A. Neuwirth et al. (eds.), *Qur'ān in Context,* Leiden: Brill, 533-536.

Mir, Mustansir, 1986, *Coherency in the Qur'an,* Indianapolis: American Trust Publications

Mourad, Suleiman A., 2008, 'Mary in the Qur'an', in Gabriel Said Reynolds (ed.), *The Qur'an in its Historical Context,* Abingdon: Routledge, 163-174.

Mundadan, M.A., 1998, *Paths of Indian Theology,* Bangalore: Dharmaram Publications.

Musk, Bill, 2003, *The Unseen Face of Islam,* London: Monarch

Nawas, John A., 1996, 'The Miḥna of 218 A. H./833 A. D. Revisited: An Empirical Study', *Journal of the American Oriental Society,* Vol. 116, No. 4 (Oct. - Dec.), 698-708

Neuwirth, A, N. Sinai and M. Marx (eds.), 2010, *Qur'ān in Context,* Leiden: Brill, 2010

Nisbett, Richard, 2005, *The Geography of Thought,* London: Nicholas Brealey Publishing

Ott, B., 2001, *Beyond Fragmentation,* Oxford: Regnum Books International

Phan P (ed.), 2011, *Christianities in Asia,* Oxford: Blackwell

Rahman, Fazlur, 1980, *Major Themes of the Qur'an,* Chicago: Bibliotheca Islamica
_____ 1982, *Islam and Modernity,* Chicago: University of Chicago Press

Ramachandra, V. & Peskett, H., 2003, *The Message of Mission,* Leicester: IVP

Reichelt K., 1937, 'Buddhism in China at the present Time and the New Challenge to the Christian Church' in *The International Review of Missions* Vol. 26, 155-166
_____ 1938, 'The Johannine Approach' in *The Authority of Faith* Tambaram Series 1, 90-101

_____ 1953, *Meditation and Piety in the Far East,* Cambridge: James Clarke and Co

Reynolds, Gabriel Said (ed.)., 2008, *The Qur'an in its Historical Context,* London: Routledge

Rivers, Julian, 2011, 'Islamic Courts in the English Legal System', in Bell and Chapman (eds.), *Between Naivety and Hostility: Islam in Britain,* Milton Keynes: Authentic, 171-186.

Robinson, W.H., 1958, *The Christian Experience of the Holy Spirit,* Great Britain: Digswell Pl.

Rooy, S., 1988, 'Historical Models of Theological Education' in Padilla, R., *New Alternatives in Theological Education,* Oxford: Latin American Fraternity

Ross A, 1994, *A Vision Betrayed – The Jesuits in Japan and China,* Edinburgh: EUP

Small, Keith E., 2011, *Textual Criticism and Qur'an Manuscripts,* Lanham: Lexington Books

Sørensen, J.S., 2007, *Missiological Mutilations,* Frankfurt am Main: Peter Lang

Sorik A, 1997, 'The Cross and the Lotus' in *Areopagus* Vol. 9, No 4 (Winter/Spring) 72-7

South Asia Forum, 2011, *Jesus Through Asian Eyes,* Evangelical Alliance

Stacey, Vivienne, 1986, *Christ Supreme,* Lahore: MIK.

_____ 1995, *Women in Islam,* Interserve (available via (http://www.stfrancismagazine.info/ja/content/blogcategory/34/49/)

Stackhouse, M., 1988, *Apologia: Contextualization, Globalization, and Mission in Theological Education,* Grand Rapids: Eerdmans

Stanley B, 2012, Http://www.ed.ac.uk/schools-departments/divinity/staff-profiles/stanley (Accessed 13.03.12)

Stewart C. & Shaw R., 1994, *Syncretism/Anti-Syncretism,* London: Routledge

Strandenoes, T., 2009, 'Contextualising the Commitments and Concerns of Dr. Karl Ludvig Reichelt in the 21st Century' in *Swedish Missiological Themes* 97, 2, 127-140

Taylor, W (ed.), 1991, *Internationalising Missionary Training,* Exeter: WEF

_____ 1997, *Too Valuable to Lose,* Pasadena: William Carey

Telle N. R., 1981, 'The Legacy of Karl Ludvig Reichelt' in *IBMR* Vol. 5, 65-69

_____ 2008, 'The Gift of Being Number Two: A "Buzz Aldrin" Perspective on Pioneer Missions' in *IBMR* Vol. 32, 81-4

Thangasamy, D. A., 1966, *The Theology of Chenchiah,* Bangalore: CISRS

Thomas, P.V., 1969, 'Indian Approaches to the Knowledge of Christ' in *Indian Journal of Theology,* 18(1969), 88-99.

Tyldesley, Esther, (trans.), 2010, *Confucius From The Heart,* London: Pan Books, 2010

Bibliography

Uchimura, K , 1984, 'The Two Js' in *Uchimura Kanzo Zenshu*, Tokyo: Iwanami Shoten

Van den Toren, B., 2010, 'Can We See the Naked Theological Truth?' in Cook et al., *Local Theology for the Global Church*, Pasadena, CA: William Carey Library

Van Ess, Josef, 2006, *The Flowering of Muslim Theology*, Cambridge, Mass.: Harvard U.P.

Vargas Llosa, M., 1990, *The Storyteller*, London: Faber

Von Sivers, Peter, 2003, 'The Islamic Origins Debate Goes Public', in *History Compass* 1.

Wadud, Amina, 1999, *Qur'an and Woman:* Oxford: Oxford University Press

Walls, A., 1996, *The Missionary Movement in Christian History*, Edinburgh: T & T Clark

Wansbrough, John, 1977, *Qur'anic Studies*, Oxford: Oxford University Press

Winter, R. & Hawthorne, S.C., 2009, *Perspectives on the World Christian Movement* (4th edition), Pasadena: William Carey

Witherington III, B., 1998, *The Acts of the Apostles*, Carlisle: Paternoster Press

Wu, Joseph S., 2004, 'Basic Characteristics of Chinese Culture', in *Comprehensive Harmony: e-Journal for Comparative Philosophy and Culture*, Vol. I, No.3, Fall, 2004, http://www.thomehfang.com/suncrates3/1wu.html (accessed 18.3.2012)

Yeo, K. K., 2008, *Musing with Confucius and Paul*, Cambridge: James Clarke and Co.

RECENT REGNUM TITLES

Regnum Edinburgh Centenary Series

A Learning Missional Church: Reflections from Young Missiologists
Beate Fagerli, Knud Jørgensen, Rolv Olsen, Kari Storstein Haug and Knut
Tveitereid (Eds)
2012 / 978-1-908355-01-1 / 218pp (hardback)
Cross-cultural mission has always been a primary learning experience for the
church. It pulls us out of a mono-cultural understanding and helps us discover a
legitimate theological pluralism which opens up for new perspectives in the
Gospel. Translating the Gospel into new languages and cultures is a human and
divine means of making us learn new 'incarnations' of the Good News.

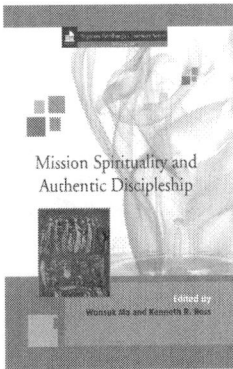

Mission Spirituality and Authentic Discipleship
Wonsuk Ma and Kenneth R Ross (Eds)
2013 / 978-1-908355-24-9 / 274pp (hardback)
This book argues for the primacy of spirituality in the
practice of mission. Since God is the primary agent of
mission and God works through the power of the Holy
Spirit, it is through openness to the Spirit that mission
finds its true character and has its authentic impact. This is
demonstrated today particularly by movements of
Christian faith in the global south which carry the good
news to the heart of communities in every part of the
world. Originating in the Edinburgh 2010 mission study
project, the essays assembled in this volume show that
today there is a renewal of the missionary impetus of the churches which is
marked by its spiritual character. Here fresh motivation for mission is being
found, moving people of faith to share the good news of Jesus Christ both within
their own communities and by crossing frontiers to take the message to new
contexts.

Regnum Studies In Global Christianity

Contemporary Pentecostal Christianity: Interpretations
from an African Context
J Kwabena Asamoah-Gyada
2013 / 978-1-908355-07-2 / 238pp

Pentecostalism is the fastest growing stream of Christianity
in the world. The real evidence for the significance of
Pentecostalism lies in the actual churches they have built
and the numbers they attract. This work interprets key
theological and missiological themes in African
Pentecostalism by using material from the live experiences
of the movement itself.

From this World to the Next: Christian Identity and Funerary Rites in Nepal
Bal Krishna Sharma
2013 / 978-1-908355-08-9 / 238pp
This book explores and analyses funerary rite struggles in a nation where Christianity is a comparatively recent phenomenon, and many families have multi-faith, who go through traumatic experiences at the death of their family members. The author has used an applied theological approach to explore and analyse the findings in order to address the issue of funerary rites with which the Nepalese church is struggling.

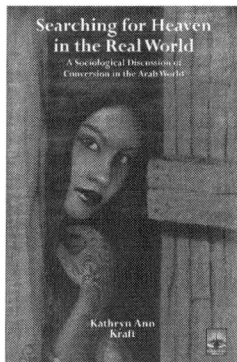

Regnum Studies In Mission

Searching for Heaven in the Real World: A Sociological Discussion of Conversion in the Arab World
Kathryn Kraft
2012 / 978-1-908355-15-7 / 1428pp
Kathryn Kraft explores the breadth of psychological and social issues faced by Arab Muslims after making a decision to adopt a faith in Christ or Christianity, investigating some of the most surprising and significant challenges new believers face.

Proclaiming the Peacemaker: The Malaysian Church as an Agent of Reconciliation in a Multicultural Society
Peter Rowan
2012 / 978-1-908355-05-8 / 268pp
With a history of racial violence and in recent years, low-level ethnic tensions, the themes of peaceful coexistence and social harmony are recurring ones in the discourse of Malaysian society. In such a context, this book looks at the role of the church as a reconciling agent, arguing that a reconciling presence within a divided society necessitates an ethos of peacemaking.

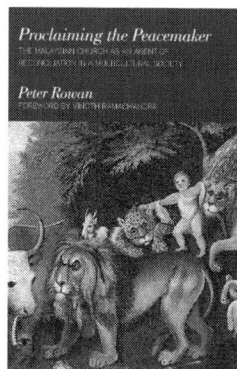

Regnum Books International

Regnum is an Imprint of The Oxford Centre for Mission Studies
St. Philip and St. James Church, Woodstock Road, Oxford, OX2 6HR
For full listing go to: www.ocms.ac.uk/regnum

regnum